Table of Contents

Introduction

My hope is that this book is different from all the other personal development books out there. As I'm writing this, I keep thinking of how long I've actually put it off; wondering if it really mattered if I wrote it with so much content already out there nowadays between books, podcasts, articles, and social media. I thought, "what's the point?" Then, I realized it's not this book that matters, it's the people it reaches. I'm sure much of what's said in this book has been said before. So why write it? Because there will be people who read this that haven't heard these things before or haven't heard them in this way, and it makes an impact in their lives. I hope that you're one of these people.

Throughout, you'll hear my personal stories, traumas, and lessons I've learned. My goal is to help you overcome/avoid the same struggles on the road to your best life. I also do not want this book to just be another dust collector on a shelf. I want it to *truly* help guide you. While I have examples and specific action steps you can take in your life, much of this book will be focused on things that you already know you should/shouldn't do, viewed from perhaps a different perspective. Unlike most books you may read, you're going to *write* in this book too! If you have dreams already or are trying to dream again, then do NOT skip the lines at the end of each chapter without writing something. This is important for memory retention, getting you thinking outside your normal thought patterns, and for review later down the road (which we'll come back to at the end).

Take your time. I designed this with simplicity so that you can take it one chapter at a time. There's 31 chapters, which are fairly short, so if you want to read a chapter a day and finish it in a month, that's fine. Just make sure you write in it and truly plan what changes you're going to make in your life moving forward. Your dream life is waiting on you.

Potholes & Speed Bumps

Potholes

Ever feel like you're cruising along in life, things seem to be going well, then you trip and nearly land on your face? That's a pothole. The longer you're on a specific road in your life, the more likely you're gonna hit a pothole. You get that awesome job, and end up with a new boss or coworker you can't stand. You get that "new to you" car, and 6 months in you start having engine trouble. You start dating that awesome person, then find out they put the toilet paper on backwards (ok, that's more of a "ROAD CLOSED" situation). With potholes, you can't do a whole lot about them, you just have to expect them and navigate them the best you can. Sometimes you're able to swerve around them, sometimes you hit them head on, and you move on down the road.

Throughout my career in the health and fitness industry, I've impacted a lot of lives. Some clients absolutely crushed it. Some quit after 2 days. I saw the potential in them, they just didn't see it in themselves yet. Nothing against those people (believe me I've had my own self doubts countless times, even in writing this book). As far as my businesses were concerned though, those situations are considered potholes. I expected those clients to continue and to do well. Sometimes, I kinda predicted they would quit, but I was often caught off guard. It shook me for a moment, then I moved on. The majority of those that quit weren't ready for potholes themselves.

People often believe that once they commit to working on their health it's going to be easy, simple, and smooth sailing. That's definitely not the case. The same goes in your career. There's always learning curves with starting a new job and mishaps beyond that. There will always be misunderstandings in our relationships as well. Ever hit a pothole on the road and just turn around to go back home? I doubt it, yet in life people do that all the time.

There will be a lot of potholes along the way to our dream lives. The thing is, they exist even if we don't work towards that dream life as well. Think about a time in your life where you've settled, where nothing has changed for years. I'm sure in that time you can think of some potholes you ran into, right? I'll definitely take the ones on the road to my dream life, and I hope you will too.

Speed Bumps

Just like potholes, speed bumps are going to happen in life; and just like on the road, they're meant to slow you down. In life, these are seen as humbling moments. You're crushing it in your career, getting promotions, raises, and praise, and you think nothing can go wrong. Then, you mess something up and get written up or yelled at by your boss. You're running your own company and business is soaring, then it takes a dip and you have to reevaluate some things. You're closer than ever with your significant other, then you screw up and get in a big argument and have to sleep on the couch. You're crushing it in your health journey, then you have an injury that sets you back a while. We need speed bumps in our lives, and oftentimes these are actually learning moments where we can course-correct and be more prepared for the next pothole or speed bump that may come along.

A speed bump for me recently was tweaking my back. Fortunately, it wasn't too bad and only had me missing workouts for a couple weeks, but I had been getting back into a solid routine when it happened. I've had many speed bumps over the years in my health journey. They all remind me to listen to my body, do not overdo it, and keep pushing forward. When it comes to health, in fact, I believe speed bumps are quite possibly the main cause of why people quit. People often feel once they get started it's going to be smooth sailing. That's never the case. There will be numerous speed bumps along the way, and remember that you're on your health journey the rest of our life (whether you're focused on it or not).

Another big speed bump for me was when I first applied to become a Personal Training Manager. Up until that point, I had never been turned down after an interview. I had already done really well as a personal trainer and thought I had it in the bag. I got turned down, not even making it to the final round of interviews, and it hit me pretty hard. I was so upset I became bitter for a while about it until I realized it wasn't the end, I'd survive, and I could apply again. About six months later, in fact, I applied and finally got it! They put me in one of the smallest gyms, which was definitely a rebuild, and I built a team then went on in my second full year to be one of the top two gyms in the company of 24 locations for growth! I'm actually glad I got rejected that first time. I needed that gut check and I truly believe it made me a better manager.

Speed bumps are an important part of life. Sometimes we need that gut check so we don't further land on our face.

What potholes have you been running into and how are you navigating them?

____

____

What's a recent speed bump that humbled you?

____

____

What's an area of life you feel you're crushing it and how are you prepared for a pothole or speed bump?

____

____

Expressways & Cruise Control

You're closer than ever to your significant other, you're at your peak in your career and still climbing, your health is at an all time high, and you're even finding time for your favorite hobbies and hanging out with friends. This is the expressway. We get in that groove where life (at least for this moment) seems easy. Everything is moving as you expect, and you feel like you're flying. We wish life were always like this, though we know expressways aren't forever, and at some point we gotta accept more challenges (getting over and taking an exit) to move to the next stage of our journey.

The first time I was a personal trainer in a gym, I got to a point where my schedule was full, I was changing tons of lives, I was doing well financially, and I had a pretty awesome schedule. It definitely felt like the expressway. I knew I wanted change though. I wanted to become a Personal Training Manager. I had to exit the expressway and pass my clients off to other trainers so I could transfer to another gym to oversee a team of personal trainers. The transition wasn't easy (I'll get to that more, too), but eventually I reached another expressway. I grew that gym to be one of the only two gyms (out of 24) in the company that showed a profit that year while also training a handful of clients myself *and* managing a rockstar team I built. Then what happened? I had to exit that expressway again when I was offered another gym to fix. There will be expressways in life. You gotta put the work in to get to them and always remember they're never permanent. Each one will help you get to the next one, though.

No More Cruise Control

On the road, when we're going to be on the expressway or highway for a while, we often set the cruise control, zone out, and listen to music. It can be *really* relaxing! There's seasons in life when we may do that too, and that's totally ok. Honestly, I could probably benefit from doing that more often (as I'm constantly overthinking). The issue arises when we set the cruise control in life *too* much. I see this often with people who are just going through the motions in life, yet barely surviving. Again, we all have seasons in life, but if you set the cruise control for too long and you're only going 30 miles per hour on the highway, everyone (including life) is going to pass you by. You may run out of time before you can make it to your dream life.

When we're in survival mode, it's ok to set the cruise for a short time. How long depends on what you need and what's going on in your life. I can't set an exact time frame, only you can. Just keep your dreams in mind, and do not let survival mode completely derail you for too long. Much of my road to my dream life actually started in the last five years or so. Before that, I didn't really dream much, and any goals I had for life were pretty short-term. When it came to long-term goals outside of raising a family, I had no idea what I wanted and often did the bare minimum. Yes, I still accomplished things, but looking back I had the cruise control set *way* too often. I've grown more in the past five years than I had my entire adult life before then. I spent way too much time in survival mode.

When we're on the expressway, we can have the cruise control set too long as well! The first self help book I ever read was *The Slight Edge* by Jeff Olson. I honestly hated reading most of my life until I read that book and it talked about reading just 10 pages per day. I thought, "I'm a slow reader, but I can do that." I was leading a team of personal trainers at the time, and I committed to reading a book a month for quite some time to learn to be a better leader and impart the knowledge onto my trainers. It went *really* well! I didn't realize how much it would change *me* as well though. If this is your first self help book you've read, first I want to thank you for taking the time to read it. Secondly, do not stop with this one. There's a ton of amazing books out there, and you'll find a list of some at the end of this book that I've read so far. Back to cruise control, in that book he touched on this as well. When we're on the expressway of life and we set the cruise, we sometimes ignore the things that got us there in the first place. Our lives are built by our habits, both good and bad. This applies even in our health journey. It's why we have to exercise and eat healthy our entire lives if we want to live our best lives. Even the fittest bodybuilder will get out of shape if they stop exercising and eating healthy long enough. When you're crushing it, always remember what got you there in the first place.

What areas of your life feel like expressways right now?

____

____

Success leaves clues. What are you doing to keep the above areas on the expressway, and how can you apply these habits to other areas of your life?

____

____

When you're in survival mode, what's your baseline action steps you can take that will still move you forward in some way?

____

____

When you're on the expressway, what habits are you keeping up to make sure you stay there longer?

____

____

Distractions & Attractions

Distractions

Along the road to your dream life, there's going to be a lot of distractions. These can be both positive and negative. Let's talk about the positive distractions first.

Sometimes, you have to stop and smell the flowers. If you stay on the highway your whole life and never look at the scenery, the drive can get pretty boring. You may even fall asleep (which is a whole other issue). Stopping to smell the flowers may be using some of your savings to go on a vacation, splurging a little on something you really want on Black Friday, going out on a fancy date night, or taking a week off from building your business to just enjoy family time.

A positive distraction for me is superhero movies and shows. Do not make me choose between DC and Marvel though, I can't. My favorite superheroes in order are Superman, Captain America, Batman, and Spiderman. I have my opinions on individual movies and shows from both sides, of course, but overall I just love watching them. They bring me joy and often inspire me.

Now let's talk about negative distractions. You've heard of rubbernecking right? You see an accident on the road, and can't help but stare at it as you pass by. The problem is this sometimes causes more accidents, which would obviously slow down your journey. Negative distractions are the things that directly hinder your path to your dream life. If you're really focused on losing weight and eat a whole pizza, that's a negative distraction. If you keep telling yourself that you need to apply for that job but keep binging Netflix instead, that's a negative distraction. Here's where it gets complicated. Oftentimes distractions can be either positive or negative, depending on how much they slow you down. Even if they hinder you in the moment, as long as you get right back on the road, they can sometimes help you go faster once you're back at it. Again, we can't stay on the highway forever.

For me, unhealthy food can be both a positive and a negative distraction. If I'm crushing my health goals and have a piece of pizza or a cookie (yes it's still unhealthy), but if I get right back on track and it helps me stay focused otherwise, then that's a positive. If it causes me to fully derail (which has happened many times), then that's a negative. I've been on both sides of it, just like everyone. I've just learned to stay on the positive side much more often than the negative side.

Remember, the action needs to match the goal. The more urgent your timeline for your goals are, the more important it is to stay the course. If you're wanting that promotion asap, turn off Netflix and study for that certification. If you're wanting to lose that weight by your birthday coming up fast, put the cookie down (I hope you heard that in

Arnold's voice and got the reference), eat the salad, and get to the gym.

Attractions

Attractions are the little wins along the way. On a road trip, of course we have somewhere we're trying to get to, but it doesn't mean we can't enjoy the journey. Part of that is checking out things along the way. On the road to your dream life, it's the small wins that help keep you going. If your whole trip was all about the destination and just driving through corn fields, it would get pretty boring and feel like it's taking forever. Small wins help break it up and keep you motivated on the destination.

Back in 2013, I married the love of my life. My dad surprised us by paying for our dream honeymoon to Disney World. This was when we lived in Missouri, long before moving to Orlando. The drive was intense (my wife didn't want to fly at the time), but we enjoyed the road trip. Before we left, my wife had already planned a little surprise. Apparently Metropolis, IL was on the way to Disney World, and I'd never even heard of it nor known what was there! When she told me where we were headed first, I'm pretty sure I screamed like a little girl. Seeing that giant Superman statue was incredible!!! Unfortunately, the stores weren't open when we went because it was too early and we had to get back on the road, but we've been back since then with our boys (Clark and Bruce btw, yes named after Superman and Batman) and it's definitely a core memory for all of us now. It's probably the best surprise attraction I've ever had!

In your health journey, if your goal is to lose 100lbs, 5lbs may not seem like a lot but taking a moment to celebrate those wins helps and it IS a big deal! I always celebrate the NSVs (non scale victories) as well. At the end of the day, it's not about weight loss, it's what you can get out of life by not carrying around the extra weight. In your career, perhaps you have a long term goal, and on that path it requires multiple promotions, time spent in the industry, or accolades. Those are all attractions to enjoy as well.

I remember when I first started training in kenpo (a form of karate that's more focused on self defense and real world scenarios than competing). I had just finished college for the 2nd time and had been in school consistently since kindergarten. I didn't know what to do with my time so I decided to take up martial arts. I was single at the time. At first, I had no idea how far I would take it, but it wasn't long before I decided I wanted to earn a black belt. Along the way to get there, I had to earn orange, purple, blue, green, and 3 brown belts first. It took extensive and intense training, but 3.5yrs later I earned my black belt then went on to earn my 4th degree black belt. I'll never forget the day I earned my black belt and how stoked I was, but on the path to get there I also celebrated all those other belts. If I didn't, I don't know that I would've stuck it out. There aren't a lot of people that make it to black belt, and there would be a lot less if that was the only rank you could earn. The small wins along the journey are incredibly important and part of the memories you'll cherish.

Now, when these small wins happen, how do we celebrate them? Obviously to truly appreciate them we have to take a moment, right? This could literally be a few minutes of mental gratitude or a vacation (depending on how big the small win is). Regardless of what it is, make sure your celebration isn't the opposite of your win. I'll give you an example that's actually quite common. Suppose you lost five or ten pounds and your goal is 50 pounds. That's a great accomplishment, and something you should be proud of. You could celebrate by buying smaller clothes, buying some other item you promised yourself once you reached that small goal, get a pedicure, or just tell some supportive loved ones so they can congratulate you as well. Something that people do often though is "reward" themselves with their favorite junk food (like pizza, fast food, donuts, etc). This is exactly what you do NOT want to do. It's the opposite of your small win, and encourages an unhealthy relationship with food. Eating healthy is rewarding yourself and eating junk is cheating yourself, not the other way around. Make sure how you enjoy your attractions isn't deterring you from your dream life.

What positive distractions have you had lately?

____

____

What negative distractions have you faced lately?

____

____

What will you do to overcome the negatives in the future?

____

____

What small wins have you experienced or are you experiencing on your journey?

____

____

How are you taking time to celebrate and truly enjoy them without deterring you from getting back on the main road?

____

____

What's an attraction you've been wanting to experience but have been putting off?

____

____

Set a date right now. When will you make it happen?

___/___/____

What do you need to do to prepare to make it happen on that date?

____

____

Wrong Turns

We've all made wrong turns on the road, and when chasing our dreams it's no exception. Wrong turns are inevitable. Sometimes we actually need them to understand it's not the way we need to go. There's even times they turn out to be a shortcut, or we find a new store we wanna check out. In life, these can be relationships that don't turn out like we expected, careers or jobs we discover we don't enjoy, places we move to where we end up hating the community or weather, or finding new friends only to discover you do not get along or have anything in common.

I've made many wrong turns in life. Before I met the love of my life, I was actually engaged to another woman. I won't go into detail, but it definitely didn't end well and I ended up having to cut her completely out of my life. I've graduated college three times with different degrees. Before I got into the fitness industry, I was a Data Analyst for a marketing research company for over seven years sitting behind a desk punching code. No judgment if you do something similar and love it, it just wasn't for me. It turned out to be a wrong turn.

There's another aspect of wrong turns that we need to discuss. Ever make a wrong turn on the road and you're convinced that you'll still get to your destination, so you keep driving, only to put yourself even further from where you wanna go? It's ok, I'm guilty of it too. When we realize a choice we made in life is a wrong turn, it's important to change direction as soon as we can. Life is too short to stay on the wrong path for too long. We all know people who have worked the same job they hate for less pay than they need or deserve for decades, waiting for retirement only to have no money and poor health when that time comes to actually do anything. Unfortunately, I know this happens quite often.

My dad was a welder most of his working years, then he worked in factories towards the end before he retired. Not long after, he decided that he wanted to go back to work part time. He applied for welding and factory jobs, but because of his age and his hearing (he's been mostly deaf for most of his life), he had a hard time finding work. I told him to apply for other types of jobs but he was reluctant, thinking after all these years he couldn't do anything else. Finally, he started applying for things outside his comfort zone, and now he actually works in in-home health taking care of elderly who can't take care of themselves. Most of the time he just keeps them company, but he loves it and he's told me many times he never thought he'd be doing something like this. Even when he was in the hospital recently, he told me he couldn't wait to get out because he wanted to get back to his clients.

Now, before I mentioned short cuts or stores you want to check out. Do not get discouraged if you've made some wrong turns or you're currently on one. Sometimes, wrong turns turn out to be a blessing in disguise. As you change course, do not burn any bridges. Sometimes the people you met could come back around in life and you could benefit each other in some other way. They may know someone in your new field of work, be familiar with your new hobby or interest and give advice, or you may even start dating a past coworker or someone you went to college with. Life often comes full circle. Keep those connections, and do not forget the skills you've learned, even on the wrong roads.

After being in the fitness industry over 10 years, I've impacted a lot of lives. A lot of them I met in the gym, but I've also helped a lot of people I grew up with (many of whom I barely spoke to growing up). I've helped people I worked with in past jobs, and as I've switched companies in the fitness industry, I've had many clients follow me or try out new avenues I've used so that I could help them even more.

When it comes to skills, I never realized how much having an IT background would help me in the fitness industry. It's helped tremendously with programming for clients digitally, staying organized (which allows me to help more people), and many of the documents I've created have been used at numerous gyms and in multiple companies. When I was a personal training manager, they even had me traveling around to different locations in the company to show other managers how to use what I created and be more organized.

If you know in your gut you're still traveling down a wrong turn, this is your sign. It's not too late to go another way! Just do not forget all you've learned and the connections you've made. They may just be exactly what you need for the next road in your life.

What's a wrong turn you've made that you're still traveling?

____

____

What can you do today to course correct?

____

____

What's something you've learned from a past wrong turn that helped you now?

____

____

As you adjust and course correct, what knowledge and connections will you keep up that will help on this new part of your journey?

____

____

Traffic

That word alone may make you stressed and irritated. No one says "I love traffic!". When it comes to fighting for our dream life, traffic is similar. It's people in the way (I'll get to construction later). Everyone is trying to get to their destinations, too, and things can get clogged up. It may be others going for the same job as you. It may be that person you want to be the love of your life dating others instead. It could be gym traffic when the gym is too crowded for you to use the equipment you planned on. You can also think of traffic as competition if you own a business or play a sport.

Some traffic that I've run into is in the fitness industry. We always focus on being a *team* of personal trainers, but at the end of the day, there's only so many people in the gym and only so many trainers. So what do we do? When it comes to car traffic, there isn't much unless we can figure out a different work schedule or work from home. It's possible, though! In life, we may have more options. Make yourself stand out. As a trainer, I make it a point to try and work harder than everyone else. I also use my martial arts background with my clients because most other trainers do not know that skillset. When I was a PT manager of a small gym for a company of 24 locations, my goal was to always have the most client successes with my team than anyone else's.

In those interviews, what sets you apart as a strength to that company? With that potential love of your life, what can you do to get their attention that no one else is doing? In the gym, can you move your schedule around so you can go when it's less crowded? If you own a business, how can you market better or find more of a niche to set yourself apart from your competition?

There's one other way we can deal with traffic, even though it's no one's favorite. Wait it out. Obviously traffic clears up eventually on the road, and you get to your destination, right? In nearly any job I've worked, if I worked there long enough (and often only a couple years), I became a veteran employee. A lot of jobs have a high turnover rate. Often, that's a bad sign, but if you truly enjoy the job and want to climb the corporate ladder there (aside from making yourself stand out and going above and beyond helping others and your bosses), you can simply play the waiting game. If you work hard and stay consistent, there's a high probability that you'll get promoted or get more raises. You often get to a point where you become indispensable, and at that point you have more pull.

Now, here's the caveat with this option: it's not always guaranteed that you'll advance. You may get stuck in one lane while others are passing you in another. It also may be too long of a wait and you have places to be, right? If you keep getting passed up or it's taking too long AND you're always learning, growing, and going above and beyond, it may be time to move on and get on another road to get to where you wanna go. First, I would sit down and have a discussion with your boss to figure out if there's an issue you're not seeing. If not, look for another job. Often, one of the best ways to improve your income and advance in your career is switching jobs. Many places may not give you the promotion or raise you want simply because they like you where you are and don't think that you'll actually leave. If you're stuck in traffic too long and your ETA is far longer than what you want, it may be time to change roads to get there faster. We'll discuss this more later.

Side Note: For dealing with actual traffic, which we'll discuss more later as well, listen to a podcast or audio book based on your weaknesses or things you want to learn! Make the most of that time, and you may actually enjoy being stuck in traffic more! Remember, we all have the same 24 hours in a day, and the most successful people utilize it more efficiently. I guarantee most of the others in the traffic of your life aren't listening to podcasts and audiobooks to work on their weaknesses.

Overcoming life traffic often isn't easy, but once you find ways around it, you can typically get moving much faster!

What's some life traffic that you're running into?

____

____

How can you navigate it better?

____

____

Accidents

Accidents on the road happen all the time, and in life it's no exception. I'm mainly talking about the ones that involve us. Let's first discuss the accidents we cause. As a teenager and in my early 20's, I actually rear ended numerous cars on the road from falling asleep at the wheel. I didn't learn until years later that it was actually due to my horrible nutrition at the time. In life, I've caused many accidents as well. We've all said the wrong thing to someone, did something we thought was right yet ended horribly, messed something up at work and got in trouble, etc. Pretty much every client I've ever had has messed up in their health journey at some point, which is part of the journey.

So, what do we do about it? Well, we often can't change the accident. What's done is done. The good thing is that we can use our accidents as an opportunity to learn, adapt, and move forward more intelligently so they're less likely to happen again. Back in high school, I can easily think of a couple accidents that I caused. Once I started driving, I made a game out of passing all nine school buses on this straight part of the road. I'd hit some pretty fast speeds in my old car. One time, I saw a semi truck up ahead pulled over on the side of the road, but no other cars, so I went for it. Turns out that as I got closer, that semi wasn't on the side of the road and it was headed right for me! I had to take the ditch, go through two yards, and nearly take out a couple mailboxes. Fortunately, no one was injured, a lot of people that saw it yelled at me the next day, and I learned to never do that again.

Another instance, I was working at a movie theater and messed up my schedule so it overlapped with a school trip for JROTC that I had signed up for. No one could cover my shift, so I simply didn't show up and got fired. I learned to never no-call no-show again. That should've been a no-brainer, but I had to learn the hard way.

Now, let's discuss accidents caused by others that impact us. As we know, this happens all the time as well. A coworker makes a mistake on a report that causes you more work, a loved one accidentally tells one of your secrets to someone or blabs about a surprise party, your kids or spouse eat the meal you prepared that was supposed to help you stay on your health journey, or someone dropped your favorite coffee mug.

All these things and more can really get under our skin and ruin our whole day or week. Or can they? Sure, if someone rear ends you on the highway, or worse, that's seriously going to impact your mood. When it comes to life accidents though (depending on the severity), we can have more control over how we react and respond. Remember, there's only two things that we have control over: our own thoughts and our own actions, and only in the present. You'll get through that extra work, that surprise party will still be fun, you can prepare another healthy meal and get right back on track, and you can get another coffee mug. For the vast majority of the accidents that happen to us, we can learn to let go of and move on.

Wow, how's this for an example? I write this paragraph as I'm going back through and editing this book, because yesterday morning I was drying my favorite coffee mug (the very first thing I bought when we moved to Florida, which had my name on it), and the handle snapped off, which caused it to fall to the floor and shatter. I admit, I was pretty upset yesterday. Sure, I could find an identical mug, but it wouldn't have the same sentimental value. Today, I realized that I have to just move on. I can't change the past, and there's nothing to really learn from this scenario to prevent it in the future. I just need to let it go.

I made a pretty huge mistake when I first got that IT job years ago. The actual mistake was relatively easy to make, but the impact potentially cost the company thousands. I thought for sure I would be fired and my mind spiraled into how my life would be radically changed. Fortunately, I was able to keep my job and learn from that mistake, so it didn't happen again. We put new safeguards in place for checking for errors. As time went on, I looked back and realized that had I lost my job, it wouldn't have been the end of the world. I would've gotten another job and figured it out. Sure, who knows where that would have led me, but we can't predict or dwell on that. Accidents happen. When you learn from them, they can (in a way) be viewed as a win.

I've had many accidents happen from others that impacted my job there as well during the seven years that I worked there. Numerous times, I had to do extra work because someone else screwed up. It was nearly a weekly occurrence. What happened? I still got paid. I still got the job done. I survived. And I moved on with my life. At the time, I had become very stressed, negative, and bitter. Looking back, I realize that I allowed those times to take up too much of my mental energy. It was a blip in my life. Remember the 5 by 5 rule: if it won't matter in 5 years, do not spend more than 5 minutes worrying about it. Also, this is something that I first heard from Ed Mylett: "Worry doesn't take away tomorrow's troubles, it takes away today's peace."

What can you learn from accidents that you've caused to move forward more intelligently?

____

____

What accidents have others caused which impacted you that you need to let go of and move on (Note: This may sometimes mean letting go of the person too if you can't forgive them, family included)?

____

____

Tolls

Growing up in Missouri, we didn't have tolls. That was a new thing to deal with when we moved to Florida. I often try to avoid them, especially if it only means a delay for a couple minutes. In life, tolls are investments that you have to make, and I do not mean just financial. Tolls are putting in the work in the gym to build muscle and burn calories. Tolls are choosing the healthy food over the junk at a restaurant or the grocery store. Tolls are having that hard conversation with loved ones about something they're doing that goes against your morals and dreams. Tolls are going the extra mile at work to please your boss because you know it's going to pay off in the long run.

I may have lived in Missouri my first 35 years of life, but I've paid a lot of tolls. I put in that extra work at numerous jobs, and it helped me advance my career. I put in the work in the gym and kitchen to become fitter than ever. I've had to call out family members for things they were doing to others. Tolls are an important part of life. Often, when I finish a workout, I think, "Dues paid, investment made." You could also say, "Tolls paid, investment made".

On the road, tolls are pretty easy to pay. Here in Florida, we have something called the Sun Pass. One of the biggest perks is that when you're on a toll road, there are lanes where you don't even have to slow down. It takes a picture, then pulls from the account that you have set up or bills you. In life, tolls are typically much more challenging. Putting in that extra work, going to the gym when you would rather sleep in, going to bed on time when you'd rather go out drinking, having that hard conversation with a loved one, or saying yes to meal prep and no to fast food can be *tough*!

The road to our dream lives is full of tolls, and unlike on an actual road, there's no getting around them. People often try to take shortcuts and end up just wasting their time and not getting to where they want to be. Pay the tolls.

What tolls are you paying that are moving you forward?

____

____

What tolls do you need to start paying?

____

____

Construction

There are always roads under construction, just like our lives are always under construction. Even when we're moving along towards our dreams as expected, small tweaks have to happen. Sometimes those tweaks are minor and just make us switch lanes, but sometimes they take more effort and really slow us down.

Construction in our lives can be as simple as changing up our morning and evening routines, or more complicated like switching jobs or careers. Think of construction like habit change.

Another major construction area is raising kids. We have two young boys, and as you know they don't come with instruction manuals like a car does. We can listen to others and read books, but most of the time it feels like we're just making things up as we go along. Everyday presents its own amazing moments and challenges. We're constantly making tweaks and finding out what works to keep things running as smoothly as we can. When it comes to parenting, the "Under Construction" sign is always up.

There's also always construction in our health. People often strive for maintenance in their health journey. I have news for you, there is no maintenance. Our bodies are constantly changing. Cells are dying and replicating every moment of every day. In fact, your skin cells are replaced every few weeks. Yep, *new* skin! Roads have wear and tear, and so do our bodies. To keep it from breaking down as fast, we have to do construction. We have to exercise, eat healthy, drink water, and get good sleep to keep the body functioning as best it can. I'll talk more about this later. Do not be the construction worker standing on the side of the road doing nothing when it comes to your health. Get to work.

What construction are you dealing with right now?

____

____

What construction do you need to implement in your habits (career, relationships, eating, drinking, sleeping, etc)?

____

____

How Long is the Road?

This is a great question. When it comes to a road trip, nowadays we just punch the destination into our GPS and it'll tell you about how long it will take to get there (and how many miles it will be). We can't do that when it comes to reaching our dream life. We don't know how long it will take or what may happen on the journey to interfere. If we can avoid accidents, pay the tolls when needed, watch out for potholes, and make sure we don't take too many wrong turns, we may get there faster than expected. Traffic and construction may also slow us down so much that it takes longer, or can even cause us to choose a different route.

In today's society, we want everything yesterday. It's what I call a "Microwave Society."

"It took me 10 years to gain 50 lbs. I want to lose it in two months."

"I applied for one job yesterday. Why don't I have it yet?"

"I went on one date. Why haven't I found the love of my life yet?"

We've all heard or even thought about these things before. Nothing worth having is instantaneous. In fact, it actually makes the destination more meaningful. Have you ever lived near a big attraction that people love to visit, yet you don't go that often yourself or keep putting it off? It's so easy and simple, you think you can always do it tomorrow.

When we moved from Missouri to Florida, our boys were 6 and 2 years old. We realized that we never took them up into The Arch, even though we lived about 20 minutes from it! People travel from all over the world to see it, and we passed it frequently, yet never made it a priority. Even now, we live an hour from the beach, yet we haven't been in about six months.

If you started college today and they handed you the degree tomorrow, it wouldn't really mean that much to you. In fact, it wouldn't mean much to anyone else either because everyone would have five of them. Putting in the time and work is what makes it mean something. It's also what sets you apart from those that aren't willing to do what it takes to reach their dreams.

The road to our dream lives isn't a 10 minute drive, and that's a good thing! It's a long road full of twists, turns, and obstacles; but believe me, the destination is worth it. Be urgent in your action and patient in the result. Celebrating the small wins (attractions) along the way really helps too! The tortoise beat the hare, right?

Play the long game, but do not let that cause you to procrastinate. The time will pass regardless, what you do with it is up to you. Ever notice on the road how the road behind you looks smaller in the rear view mirror than the road ahead of you? In life, the past often seems a lot shorter than the future. In the moment, sometimes things may seem to drag on. When we look back over our past, it often seems like it flew by in an instant. We wonder what we did with all that time, and get depressed about the time we may have wasted. When we look to the future, we often have this notion that we have plenty of time to put the work in and reach our goals. It's ok if we push them off another day, right? Do not allow tomorrow to become the thief of today. This is where a lot of people mess up.

Now, imagine you're in a helicopter looking down on your journey to your dream life. You see the past road, present road, and future road all at once. From this perspective, as you see your car driving down the road, you can realize that the time passes at the same rate. The last 10 years have the same amount of time as the next 10 years.

We don't have an address that we can just plug into a GPS to determine what time we'll arrive at our dream life, but we can set dates then reverse engineer them to determine the action steps we need to take DAILY to get there, starting TODAY!

What's a dream of yours that you can realistically accomplish in the next year?

____

____

What's a dream of yours that you can realistically accomplish in the next 10 years?

____

____

Destination Pictures

Before we go on a road trip, I'd imagine that all of us look up pictures of where we're headed first (unless it's just someone's house). We look up the attractions, beaches, scenery, restaurants, etc. We can picture being there. When it comes to our dream lives, it can be a little more challenging.

Perhaps part of your dream life involves living in a vacation spot. In that scenario, you can look up pictures of that spot and envision living there. In fact, I highly recommend it. Even print out pictures and put them on a cork board where you'll see them all the time. What's harder is looking up the exact house you want to live in, because it may not be for sale when you're ready or in the exact spot you want. I'm guessing you can't just look up a picture of the love of your life you want to marry someday, either (unless you're already with them). You definitely can't look up pictures of your future kids, since you don't have them yet.

All that being said, find pictures of what you can. Print out pictures of a monument or famous attractions of where you want to live, a house that's similar to the one you want, perhaps a logo of the company you'd like to work for, the car you want to own, a generic picture of a family if you don't have a spouse or kids yet, inspiring people you'd like to meet, and hobbies you'd like to pick up. These are just some examples. Sure, it won't be exact like destination pictures for a road trip, but just like those motivate you to keep driving, these pictures will help you keep your eyes on the road to your dream life.

There will be many days that you don't want to keep putting in the work. You wanna take the easy route. Gosh, it would seem so much easier if you just settled. Everyday, especially on those days, take a couple minutes and stare at that cork board. I've heard it called a vision board, a dream board, and a future board. Stare at it and remind yourself why you're doing what you're doing. In fact, stare at it as a family. If you have a spouse and kids at home, they're on the road to your dream life with you, right? All of you looking at that board everyday helps you focus and work together to make those things you posted on there become reality!

For those of you that have kids, especially young ones, this board can change their lives significantly. Not only are they part of all your adventures toward your dream life, it shows them they can do the same. Imagine they grow up constantly looking at a board of pictures of things you want or goals that you want to achieve in life. When they grow up, they're going to want to do the same thing! In fact, if your kids are a little older, I recommend adding a couple things they want as well and give them action steps to achieve them. This will teach them to fight for their dreams and put in the work early on!

What are some destination pictures you'd like to print out (remember - this isn't just places, it also includes life goals, material things, and hobbies/experiences)?

____

____

Get a cork board this weekend if you don't have one and start adding pictures. After you read this book, I recommend *Hustle Believe Receive* by Sarah Centrella. She goes into a lot more detail about this.

Stay in Your Lane?

You've probably heard this phrase at some point in your life. When it comes to being on the road, you obviously don't want to be swerving into other peoples' lanes. When it comes to the road to your dream life, it's a little more complicated.

When is staying in your lane a good idea? I honestly don't remember where I heard it but something I repeat often is "comparison is the thief of joy." Comparing ourselves to others who we view as doing better than us can drag us down and demotivate us. Comparing ourselves to others who we view as worse off than us can cause us to settle for a life less than we want or deserve. If you're going to compare yourself to anyone, compare yourself to the person you were 24 hours ago. Why only 24 hours ago? If 20 or 30 years ago you played professional basketball or ran marathons, and now you've had two knee replacements, getting back to that may not be an option. You can't change the past. Focus on getting just 1% better each day, and you'll go far in life.

I admit, I've had a bad habit of getting into comparison mode most of my life when it comes to fitness and building muscle. I grew up very scrawny, got bullied in school, always got picked last for sports, and always felt alone, even around friends. The last thing I wanted to do was stay in my lane because I didn't love myself. I got into lifting weights in high school and loved it. In my mind, this was the answer. If I built a bunch of muscle, I would love myself more, and others would love me more. This is NOT the way to find self love or love from others; yet, unfortunately, I feel like this is actually a common thought process. It took a lot of trial and error with some results until I ultimately went to school for personal training and learned how to actually build muscle properly. Even then, I was still stuck in comparison mode. Once I was in a gym for a long time, it was never good enough. There's always someone bigger to compare to.

While I didn't go to therapy (I highly recommend it, though), I've read a lot of books, listened to a lot of podcasts, done a lot of self reflection, and had coaches and mentors that have helped me a lot with it. I still have my moments, but I have more love for myself now than I ever have and now my goals are about me and no one else. In fact, I'm in the process right now of building more muscle; but this time, it's to be Bane from Dark Knight Rises for Halloween. I realize that still sounds like comparison, but it's because I just want to look the part and I realize that I have tons of self worth regardless of my size.

When is staying in your lane a bad idea? An important part of life is staying open-minded. We shouldn't stop learning after high school or college. We have an incredible gift for learning, and not a single person has reached the height of what the human brain is capable of. No matter how long you've been married, been working on your health journey, been in college, or been in your career, there is ALWAYS more to learn. Spending time in other peoples' lanes to learn from them will take you further in life than anything. We are better together.

I just mentioned all those books I've read and podcasts I've listened to, and this is why. We've all heard knowledge is power, and it's completely true! It gives you power over your own life. Staying open-minded and willing to learn is an important part of the road to your dream life. If you're on a long road trip that you've never been on before, you don't have the whole route memorized (especially if there's traffic, detours, and construction you have to deal with). You're going to have to change lanes a lot! Your dream life doesn't require the person you are now, it requires the person you'll become through learning and growing.

Throughout my years in the health and fitness industry, I've learned a lot and still learn new exercises, techniques, nutrition and habit tips, and other ways to help others. There's *always* more to learn. My wife suffers from ADHD, anxiety, and depression. I don't have those things, so I've read books and listened to podcasts about it all to better understand and communicate with her. We've struggled with finances many times in the past, so I've read books on that and taken courses on it to be better. I also want to eventually be fluent in Spanish, German, and as close with Japanese as I can get. I'd also love to learn how to fly a plane. I don't know exactly where I'll end up in life, but I'm enjoying the journey of learning and growing.

So, who's lanes do you get into? Those that have things you want. Those that have the career you want, the happiness in their relationship that you want, the finances you want, the car or house that you want, the fit body you want, or the hobbies that you want. Surround yourself with people who encourage you while also helping you strive to be better. Think of their lane as the fast lane.

In what ways do you have a bad habit of comparing yourself to others?

____

____

In what ways can you act today to make your tomorrow self better than today?

____

____

Who do you need to be around more to inspire and help you on the road to your dream life?

____

____

I Set the Path, You Set the Pace

I say this to my clients nearly everyday. As a mentor, coach, personal trainer, husband, father, friend, coworker, author (wow that's a weird feeling since this is my first book), etc., I can only listen and give guidance. It's up to the other person to put in the work. Same goes for this book. Again, my intent isn't for you to read this then just let it sit on a shelf and go back to how things have always been. My intent is for this book to help guide you on the road to your dream life. I have the questions at the end of each chapter to use as a time of reflection and a moment to decide what action steps you're going to take moving forward. I can set the path, it's up to you to determine the pace. Just like on the road when you're using your GPS, it can give you the path and even predict what time you'll arrive, but it can't predict how fast you're going to drive. If you drive like a granny (like me), it'll take longer than expected. If you drive like my wife, you'll get there faster and probably with a higher heart rate.

I always ask my clients what their timeline is for reaching their health goals. I also explain the bigger the change, the bigger the result. If they have massive goals that they want to accomplish in a relatively short amount of time, we may need to completely overhaul their nutrition and exercise right away. If they have more time, we may make small changes overtime that are easier to adopt. Either way, the action has to match the goal.

Aside from health goals, the two most important areas to set your pace are in your career and your bucket list. Where do you want to be in 5 or 10 years in your career? What position do you want to hold? What company do you want to work for? If you run your own business, how many locations do you want to run or how much profit do you want to make per year? What's on your bucket list that you've thought about for a long time, yet haven't taken any action towards? When do you want to make it happen and what will it take to get there? Work backwards on these goals to determine what you have to do daily to make them a reality, then get into action. You may have to adjust quite a few times, you may miss a few days and have to catch up, and that's ok. The important part is sticking to the date you promised yourself. The time will pass regardless. What you do with it is up to you.

Here's another great example: Today, as I'm writing this section, I decided to set a pace for this book. I determined roughly how many words I want it to include and the date I want to finish it by (at least the rough draft). Then, all I had to do was divide that to determine how many words I need to write per day. That's my pace! Because I'm one of those people that love excel, I actually put it into a spreadsheet so I can update it daily, and it'll automatically tell me my new pace and whether I'm ahead or behind.

What's one of your goals you'd like to accomplish (you may have already listed it before)?

____

____

Right now, put a date on it. When will you accomplish it? What do you have to do daily to make it a reality by that date? ___/___/____

____

____

____

____

____

____

More Than One Road

When you punch your destination into your GPS, there's often more than one path to reach it. You choose based on distance, time, tolls, other sites you may want to visit along the way, etc. The same goes in life. There's more than one path to reach your dreams, and unlike a GPS, it's very unpredictable. We don't know the exact roads we'll take, we don't know what obstacles we may face, we don't know how our dreams will change, and we don't know how long it will take to get there. Does that mean we stay where we are? I hope not!

For me, some of the biggest road changes have been in changing jobs. I've had about 15 different jobs over the years and graduated college three times. As a kid, I wanted to be a dentist, so I shadowed a dentist. After seeing a woman with black teeth get worked on, I decided that's not what I wanted to do. I also only chose it for the money. Next, I chose IT, and that one I actually pursued. After getting my Associates in General Education (which was pointless because apparently it doesn't transfer well to a tech school), I got my Bachelor's in IT and got that data analyst job. I discovered that also wasn't what I wanted to do, so I went back to college once again for personal training before finally finding my calling. I learned I love helping people win in their health, it just took me a lot of different roads to figure that out.

If you're wanting to change roads in your career, how do you even decide what road to take or how to go about it? There's a couple scenarios. First, like I did, if you're pretty confident of the path you want to take, you can go back to school. Sure, working full time and going to school at the same time will be tough. It was one of the most stressful times of my life, though it also builds work ethic and flexes your hustle muscle.

Speaking of hustle, this also brings us to the second option. If you aren't sure which path you want to choose, think about how you can make your options side hustles. I've had many side hustles over the years. I briefly started a web design company while I was working full time and going to school full time for IT. I learned pretty quickly that while I knew the code, I wasn't all that creative or artistic. I'm glad I tried it out, though! Although I went to school for it, personal training started out as a side hustle before I built the clientele to leave my desk job and a lot of trainers start out just getting a certification. I've also been part of numerous network marketing businesses, and while many of them get a bad rap, if you're with the right company, they can be quite helpful with your finances, bring you a ton of joy and flexibility, and (when it comes to health) impact a lot of lives.

Perhaps you want to start writing your own book, start a podcast, or really enjoy making videos for TikTok. Focus on what brings you joy, learn more about it, get really good at it, and you can likely over time make a lot of money at it! It may stay a side hustle, or you may wind up switching careers entirely!

Your career isn't the only place where there's multiple roads to take. Most of my life, I thought I'd always live in Missouri. I just never saw myself living anywhere else. It wasn't until my wife mentioned in passing one day that Disney was hiring (her dream job) and since I was working at home at the time with nutrition coaching, I said let's go for it! Never thought my road would take me to Florida, but here we are and I love it! She hasn't gotten that job yet due to some corporate level change-ups, but I have no doubt that she will because she's an incredible graphic designer.

A thought that crossed our minds was, "What if we don't like it or don't make it in Florida?" That's simple, we move back to Missouri or move somewhere else. Like I said before, some roads you take will be wrong turns. That's ok. Oftentimes, you have to weed out some of the roads to find the correct one.

Be flexible in the path to reach your destination, and know that you may want to change your destination as well. Also, regardless of how long you've been on a certain road, know that you can still take another one. Just because you've worked a job for decades doesn't mean it's too late to switch. We work such a huge amount of our lives, and we only get one life. Might as well enjoy it, right?

What are some alternate roads you've ended up taking in reaching your dream life?

____

____

What roads are you still considering taking moving forward?

____

____

If you're interested in starting a side hustle, what steps are you taking/will you take to move towards that?

____

____

____

____

____

____

GPS

I just talked about setting the path and the pace. There's always more than one road, and we decide how fast we travel each one. How do we know which roads to choose? In the car, we use a GPS or a map (if you're truly old school). In life, we have coaches, trainers, mentors, bosses, therapists, online professionals, authors, podcasters, and friends and family who have done what we want to do who can help guide us.

I often come across people, especially when it comes to health, who just want to do it all themselves. They'd rather fumble their way through their health journey, career, relationships, etc., than seek help. There's this odd pride, it seems, that causes people to think that they're only *truly* successful if they do it all on their own. Let's be honest, that's nonsense. It doesn't matter if you're an expert in your field, there's always more to learn. Sure, you may reach your goals and dreams on your own, but wouldn't it make more sense to do it efficiently?

I worked out consistently for 10 years on my own before I went to school for personal training. Sure, I saw some results, but it took me a lot longer. Looking back, I realize that I could've had vastly better results if I had been open to having help. We only get one life, and it flies by. We need to make the most of it, and that includes saving time. Time is the one resource that we can't get back. I often tell people: Sure, you may get to your goals by taking the backroads, but wouldn't it make more sense to take the expressway sometimes?

Also, make sure that you have the right mentors and coaches. You may not know at first, and that's the hard part. You may have to do more research and switch quite a few times. Always make sure your action matches your realistic goals. If you're following the action of your mentor, and it still isn't working, then it may be time to sit down with them and reassess the game plan or look elsewhere for guidance.

As I mentioned, when I was a kid, I decided that I wanted to be a dentist. Once I took a careers class and even a career test, I geared my answers towards being a dentist and no one questioned it. I definitely could've used some proper guidance. Once I decided that wasn't what I wanted to do and switched to IT, I went to the local community college. I decided I'd get two years of general education classes out of the way there before transferring to another college to get my bachelors. No one questioned why or if IT was the proper career for me, either. No one checked to find out if I would waste those two years because it didn't transfer to a tech school (where I told them I planned on going).

Having the correct guidance (GPS, coach, mentor, etc) is an integral part of your journey to your current and lifelong goals. Make sure that you always have some sort of guidance, and do not be afraid to change it up if you feel that the GPS is taking you the wrong way.

Now, how do you find the guidance you need? Like I mentioned, it's going to take some trial and error, but that's part of the journey. Think about people you know who already have the goals you want to achieve or are at least making progress towards them themselves. They would be the first people I talk to. They may not have all the answers, but they may be able to point you in the right direction.

If no one comes to mind, next would be referrals. Ask those you know if they know anyone with the knowledge or accomplishments that you want. They may know a good real estate agent, lawyer, personal trainer, job opportunity, or even someone single they could set you up with.

Another great source nowadays is actually social media. Posting on social media may gain you some referrals or experts in what you want from your own friends and followers who you didn't even know could help you. Posting in social media groups can help significantly as well. Depending on what you're trying to achieve, there may be groups specifically designed for it!

If those options don't work out, it may come down to researching and contacting local businesses. For instance, if you want to improve your health, finding and joining a local gym then asking for a personal trainer is a great first step. If you don't like the trainer, do not be afraid to ask for a new one from the manager. If you're needing to do some research to find the guidance you need, just make sure you research thoroughly and read reviews to save yourself some time (in case you run into some phonies or scammers).

Who's mentoring / coaching you on your road to your dream life?

____

____

In what areas of your life do you still need a mentor or coach?

____

____

What are you doing or what will you do to find them?

____

____

Are You Steering the Vehicle?

Even if you're driving down the expressway with the cruise control on, if you let go of the steering wheel, then you aren't gonna be on the road much longer. The same thing applies in life. In order to stay on the road to your dream life, you have to steer in the direction you want to go. If you let go, potholes, speedbumps, etc are going to decide where you end up, and it likely won't be pretty. We've all heard the phrase, "Jesus, take the wheel." I've never heard of someone actually letting go of the steering wheel and praying for the best going down the highway.

Do *not* pray for an easy life or for Jesus to fix everything for you. If you're a person of faith, pray for the strength to endure the challenges ahead of you and help to find a path to navigate them, then start steering.

Keeping a good grasp on the steering wheel doesn't always mean you'll choose the right roads, but it means that you're in control. Grabbing that steering wheel and taking control and full responsibility for our lives is one of the biggest advantages we can have in this life. If we allow what happens around us to control our actions or stress us out, we're only holding ourselves back from staying focused on what we can control. Even when we make those wrong turns and it's all our fault, rather than dwelling on them, we can refocus, learn from those experiences, and move on more intelligently. Do not just turn around and go home.

People often use obstacles outside their control as excuses why they can't reach their dreams as well. If you're driving and hit a pothole and it jerks your car to the left, are you going to say "oh well, let's just see what happens," or are you going to grab that steering wheel tighter and make sure you stay on the road? Grab the steering wheel of your life and do *not* let go. Even if you don't reach all your dreams, believe me, you'll end up in a much better spot than if you don't try.

What else can you control? With your significant other, it may mean owning up to how you've messed up and surprising them with a romantic dinner. In your career, it may mean showing up to work earlier, getting a new certification, going back to school, or asking for more responsibilities at work to stand out for the next promotion. In your hobbies, it may mean committing more time to Duolingo (like I'm working on as of writing this), hiring someone to teach you how to play the guitar, finally looking up martial arts studios, or taking a sewing class. In your health, it may mean signing up for a health program, joining (and GOING) to the gym three days per week, cutting back on sugar, or meal prepping.

When it comes to things outside your control that are getting in the way, we may need to take a different approach, but there's still a lot we can control. With your significant other, it may be having that hard conversation and calling them out on what's going on while also listening and trying to understand, with the end goal of coming to an agreement that you're both comfortable with. If that can't happen, in some scenarios it may mean ending the relationship. In your career, it may be having a one on one with that coworker or boss you have problems with, or even getting a new job. If there's a lot of things that bother you in your neighborhood or with your kids' school, it may be time to simply move somewhere else.

Part of what actually triggered me to finally write this book is my dad. Growing up, his biggest phrase was "Shit or get off the pot." He was recently in the hospital, and it didn't look good. We weren't sure if he'd make it home. I felt totally helpless. So I thought what CAN I do? I can take his words and use it as fuel to get started on this book, so that I can hopefully help others. In fact, as I write this paragraph, *thankfully* I can say that he's home now and actually back to work part time. Control what you can when so much seems out of your control.

Another huge area where I see people relinquishing control is in their finances. Especially nowadays, people complain about lack of pay in their job, expensive gas, food, housing, etc. We can't typically control the cost of other things aside from shopping somewhere else, but there's plenty we can control. Take charge of your budget. Track everything you spend and cut out what you don't actually need. The biggest part you can control is getting a new job. Having trouble getting one? What are you doing about it? How many jobs have you applied for? Have you thought about other lines of work? Have you considered or tried a side hustle? How many people have you asked for referrals? Have you looked into other certifications or schooling to improve your resume? Keep learning, applying, and talking to those you know that may know of a job opportunity.

Here's the harsh truth: we all have 24 hours in a day. Show me your calendar, and I'll show you your commitments. It's not a time issue, it's a priorities issue. This may mean less Netflix and more reading a book to learn about the struggles in your life, listening to more podcasts in the car on the way to work instead of music, getting up a little earlier to get a workout in, taking the time on Sundays to meal prep instead of getting fast food, or applying for more jobs instead of playing games on your phone.

For those that use time or money as the reason they can't take care of their health, squats and pushups at home are free and only take a few minutes. A basic chicken and veggie meal prepared at home can be about $2, and if you meal prep you can make nearly a whole week's worth of meals in an hour.

This isn't meant to be a guilt trip or an attack. Again, I've done these things too and still catch myself not controlling what I can. Also, remember that you can only control your thoughts and actions in the PRESENT. You can't change what you did or didn't do yesterday, or even this morning.

You also can't fully predict what you're going to do tomorrow, because that time isn't here yet. Regardless of what's happened in the past, you can take control of today better than you did yesterday.

You also may need to start small, but it's better than nothing. Read one page of a book, listen to one podcast episode, do 10 squats as you're reading this page, apply for one job today. Do something you can control today in this chaotic world, and as long as you keep that up, daily focusing on what you can control and keeping your hands at 10 and 2, you'll be amazed by how quickly your life can change for the better.

By the way, if you aren't sure what to take control of or how, and doing your own research isn't helping (there's a lot of misinformation out there), this is when you need a coach or mentor. Having a guide doesn't mean you're completely giving up control, you're just getting some guidance so that you're controlling that steering wheel in the right direction.

Let's look at some examples for what we can't control, but how we can navigate better.

You CAN'T control Aunt Suzie baking your favorite cake, but you CAN control how much you eat.

You CAN'T control whether you'll get hired for that job, but you CAN control applying and how you show up for the interview, then applying for other jobs as well.

You CAN'T control what that person did or said that bothered you, but you CAN control how you react and respond.

You CAN'T often control what time your toddler wakes up, but you CAN control what you do with that extra morning time that you didn't plan for.

One last benefit with keeping hold of that steering wheel: You can navigate mishaps from others easier, too. Imagine driving down the road, one hand on the steering wheel, somewhat distracted or zoned out, and someone cuts you off. They may nearly hit you and it freaks you out so much that you almost swerve into another car. Now, imagine that same scenario, but you're focused and your hands are at 10 and 2. You're going to be in much better control, you'll likely see that person coming over into your lane sooner, and you'll only swerve as much as you need to. When you stay focused on what you can control, people will still almost knock you off course and potholes and speed bumps will still happen; but, you'll be able to navigate them better.

Allowing the potholes, speed bumps, etc to guide the car is one of the biggest problems I see nowadays. We all know if we did that on the road, we'd end up in a ditch. Yet, we do it in life thinking we'll have a different outcome. I have news for you, you won't. You'll end up in the ditch of life. You'll be what nowadays unfortunately is "normal": unhealthy, unhappy, and broke. Do not be normal. Grab that steering wheel and do not let go!

In what areas of your life (relationships, career, hobbies, health, etc.) do you need to grab the steering wheel?

____

____

What are a couple things you've been focusing on too much that are outside your control and you need to let go of a little?

____

____

What are a couple simple things you have full control over that you can implement this week/month to take back control?

____

____

Keep Your Eyes on the Road

Aside from keeping your hands on the steering wheel, you also have to keep your eyes focused, right? Otherwise, you'll still run off the road or cause an accident. What does this look like in life? It means planning ahead and watching for obstacles that may be coming up. Just like on the road when you have to watch for cars in front of you, your next exit, or construction, you have to watch out and plan ahead for what life throws at you.

Pay attention if your significant other has seemed distant, stressed, or depressed, and try to listen to find out what's going on. If there's been layoffs at work, pay attention and try to find out how secure your job is. You may have to start looking for a new one preemptively. If you're noticing your knee is bothering you or suddenly you're weak and have no energy, you'll want to pay attention to that, too, and go get it checked out before it gets worse. Even if you feel fine and haven't gotten a checkup in a while, schedule it. I actually had a check up recently. I feel fine, but I had never really had a full checkup, and a lot of diseases run in my family. The doctor said the word "perfect" about five times (which was a huge relief), but I still plan to go back annually from now on. It's imperative to keep your eyes on the road, or you WILL end up somewhere that you don't want to be.

As you know, when you're on the road some things come up in an instant; and if you don't see them, it could mean disaster. We try our best to get around that pothole, but sometimes we still hit it. In life, some things will seem to come out of nowhere. We can't always see everything ahead of time or in time to change it. We may not see that break up, lay off, or injury coming. We may be blindsided. In those situations, we often simply have to accept them, try to learn from them, and move on.

On the other hand, we may come over a hill and see construction, traffic, or our exit far in advance. The same applies in life. We may see a potential change (good or bad) far before it happens. In these scenarios, we can often (but not always) plan ahead for them. If you're on the highway and you see traffic ahead, but there's no better route to take, at least you know you'll have to deal with it. If there's a viable exit beforehand, then you may have time to change course and take it to avoid the traffic. This is where having that long talk with your significant other, going to marriage counseling, stepping it up at work, looking for a new job, getting a doctor appointment scheduled, or hiring a physical therapist or personal trainer can come into play.

We won't catch everything in time. In fact, there's a lot that will blindside us. That's ok. Sure, those situations can be frustrating, discouraging, and demotivating. If you hit a pothole on the road, do you get so frustrated that you just take your eyes off the road and give up? No, you keep looking ahead and watch out even closer for the next one. Do the same in life. I'm not saying it'll be easy. I'm saying it'll be worth it.

I've been blindsided countless times in life. I was actually engaged to another woman before I met the love of my life, and I still remember the day when it hit me like a ton of bricks that the woman I was with wasn't the one for me. Turns out, after she'd been lying to me a ton and ended up kinda stalkerish, but that's a whole other story. Also, I was fired from two of my first jobs. The first one was as an usher and greeter at a theater, which I really loved and wanted to work there years later again (only to find out they marked me as non rehireable). The second one I was fired from was at McDonald's for being too slow on the assembly line. They referred me to another McDonald's, and I worked to become the fastest there.

I've injured my knee, nearly torn my pec, had a hernia that took out all my PTO and more for the new job I had at the time, had multiple surgeries for an abscess, and countless other spur of the moment issues. All this not counting the fact that I have two young boys, so nearly everyday I'm blindsided by something, often a toy to the face.

What do I do about all this? When I met the love of my life, I did a lot of reflection to make sure she was the one. I learned not to 'no-call, no-show' from that first job. I learned better exercise form and habits so I could reduce the risk of injury. I've read books, listened to podcasts, and I'm constantly planning ahead for the next day, week, month, year, 10 years, and even 50 years. I'm always enjoying the moment while also trying my best to be prepared for the future.

Keep your eyes on the road. Plan ahead for surprises as best you can. Regardless of the outcome, know that you at least tried to navigate it the best way you knew how at the time and with the time that you had. The vast majority of major issues we can actually see coming, and plan for better if we stay diligent and keep our eyes open.

Let's also discuss procrastination. Ever get behind someone on the road who waits until the last minute to slam on their brakes, right before hitting the car in front of them? It can be really frustrating, and nearly causes you to rear end them. Do not be that person on the road or in life. Keeping your eyes on the road doesn't do you any good if you still wait until the last minute, or it's too late to adjust course.

Waiting until your spouse storms out may be too late. Waiting until you have that surprise meeting with your boss may be too late. Waiting until the night before that term paper is due may be too late. Waiting until you're so behind on bills that your water gets shut off or you can't pay rent may be too late. Now, I'll admit that I'm guilty of procrastination sometimes too, and it's cost me many times over the years. Learn from my mistakes. You've likely run into this issue in the past. Do not forget the issues it caused.

What obstacles do you foresee coming up in your life in the next week or so?

____

____

How are you planning ahead to better navigate them?

____

____

What obstacles do you foresee coming up in your life in the next year or so?

____

____

How are you planning ahead to better navigate them?

____

____

What's a situation have you procrastinated in, and how did it impact you? Remember these times next time you see a problem or goal coming and keep wanting to put it off.

____

____

Passengers

Ever go on a long road trip alone? The sightseeing doesn't seem quite as fun, right? On the road to our dream lives, having people supporting us along the way is not only more enjoyable, it's mandatory. Sure, the passengers will swap out sometimes. Not everyone will be there to support you forever, and some of your biggest supporters you may not have even met yet. Passengers will come in the form of family members, close friends, bosses, coworkers, employees, neighbors, clients/customers, and even those on social media sometimes. For some, you'll know when their exit is, some will jump outta the car and scare you when they leave, some you may push out the door at 70mph. Regardless, passengers are an important part of your journey. They help keep you awake (focused on your journey), help you find detours when your primary path needs an alternate route, and help you create more adventures along the way.

Now, something to keep in mind that's different on the road to your dream life vs on an actual road trip: the passengers can't drive for you. On a road trip, you may swap spots so you can lay back and take a nap while they do all the work for a while. Unfortunately, that doesn't work when it comes to chasing your dreams. Passengers may support and guide you, but you still have to hold onto the steering wheel. You still have to put the work in *yourself.*

Now let's talk about the negative impact they can have, too. Think back to a time you were in the car with someone who talked your ear off about something you didn't care about, kept changing the music, or smelled funny; and you can't wait to get them outta the car. Unfortunately, these people are going to be part of your dream life journey sometimes, too. They'll distract you and cause you to lose focus, do things that mess up your progress and productivity, and overall just seem like they're messing up your mojo. They'll tell you about "shortcuts" that make it take longer for you to reach your destination, cause you to stop way more often because they have to get something, and even try to convince you that your destination is too far or too difficult to reach.

Get these people out of the car ASAP! Yes, some of these people may be family or close friends. I understand it can be difficult to break ties. If you really want to keep them around, first sit down and have a heart to heart with them. Explain what your goals and dreams are (again if you have already), explain how important they are to you, and how much you would appreciate their support. If that doesn't work, at least start cutting back on how often you see them or answer the phone. It's YOUR life and regardless of the relationship, if they're a huge detriment to you reaching your goals and dreams, it's time to truly reevaluate the relationship and how often you connect with them.

I've had plenty of both types of passengers in my life. My wife, some family, many friends, bosses, mentors, and coworkers have been incredibly supportive over the years, and I definitely wouldn't be where I am today without them! I've also had exes, family, friends, bosses, and coworkers, who weren't supportive at *all*.

Some have been integral in my successes in life. Some haven't cared at all what I do or achieve. Some have been a major source of hindrance and obstacles along the way. You're going to have a lot of passengers along your journey. Ride with the supportive ones as long as you can, and support them in their own journey too. You're better *together*. For those that are holding you back, causing accidents and unwanted detours, kick them to the curb as fast as you can!

Who's in the passenger seat that's supportive and helping you reach your dream life? Thank them today if you haven't lately.

____

____

What are their dreams? What are you doing to support them in return?

____

____

Who's in the passenger seat holding you back that you need to kick to the curb? Believe me, it may not be easy, but staying on the road to your dream life never is. Set a reminder in your phone or message them right now to at least schedule a time to chat if you want to keep in touch at least. If you'd rather fully cut ties because they're a total hindrance, and do not support you at all, do it now.

____

____

____

____

Lonely Night Time Roads

We just discussed how important having the right passengers are on your journey. Unlike during a road trip, they'll swap out many times throughout your life. Why does this happen? It's typically because someone makes a life change. You or the other person may decide to move away for a career, family member, or just the weather. One of you may start a family and between the family and working too many hours, you may drift apart. One person may even fall in with the wrong crowd, and it causes you to separate. It's not often we stay with our high school sweetheart or keep hanging out with our childhood friends.

Now, let's talk about the biggest reason you'll find some lonely roads on the path to your dream life: growth. Not everyone chases their dreams. Not everyone is willing to put the work in, fight through the struggles, and overcome the fear and challenges to reach the life they truly want. If you stay the course, you're going to have to let some people go.

Often, it's nothing against them necessarily, you may still care about them deeply. You just don't connect the same way anymore. It doesn't make either of you better than the other. You just operate at different frequencies now. They may want to continue to get drunk every weekend and spend all their time at home playing video games. In all likelihood, you have some incredible memories with them that you cherish, but that's not the life you want anymore. I'm not saying that you can never have alcohol or see them again, but getting drunk every weekend clearly isn't going to move you closer to your goals and dreams.

It can be more minor things, as well. Perhaps you have less to talk about because you're no longer keeping up on that TV show that you've both been binging. Maybe you used to go out to eat at a fast food restaurant every weekend, but you're making better eating choices and need to cut that habit out.

The person you are today likely isn't the person you'll be when you reach your dreams. The road to your dream life requires growth and change, and not everyone will join you. This can be the hardest part of the journey. Ever been on the road in the middle of the night, by yourself, on an unfamiliar road, and you started to feel scared? The same thing will happen on the road to your dream life. In fact, it will often be scary. You'll take quite a few roads you've never seen before, and many times you'll have to leave someone behind (or they'll choose to stay behind). You may not have a GPS, either. So what do you do?

Just like on the actual road, you'll navigate it the best you can, take some educated guesses, probably make some wrong turns, but eventually get to a more familiar area (or you'll drive it so much it'll become familiar and less scary). You'll realize you CAN make it; and, in fact, you'll find some great new passengers on the way that can help you get to your next destination (I'm not saying pick up more actual hitchhikers on the road though).

Becoming parents was obviously pretty scary. I still remember the day we brought our first son home and thought, "What do we do now?" We've learned as time has passed, and in the process we've lost some connections (especially with those that didn't have kids). It was just harder to connect. When I went back to school for personal training and leaving the IT industry, I ended up losing some friendships with coworkers I had known for years because we no longer had that in common and had nothing else to talk about.

Moving to Florida was probably the scariest road I've been on so far. Living my whole life in MO meant pretty much everyone I knew and was close to lived there. Leaving behind family and friends wasn't easy, but it was a choice we were willing to make so that my wife could chase her dream of working for Disney. A year and a half later, and we absolutely love Florida! We love the weather and the community and have some incredible friendships that we wouldn't have if we didn't make the plunge.

The most important part is to remember that these situations are inevitable on your journey. They may seem to come out of nowhere sometimes, but knowing they will come can help you at least mentally prepare for them. They aren't a sign that you should turn back and give up on your dream life, they're just part of the process. Push forward, you're likely closer to your dreams than you think. The life you've been dreaming of for years is more important than getting drunk on the weekends with your buddies or dropping everything to binge that show so you can talk about it. If you still want to try and keep those people around, find new ways to connect, talk to them about their own dreams, and see how you both can grow together, otherwise you're bound to grow apart.

What's a scary or lonely road of life you've been on that you're glad you pushed through?

____

____

What was better on the other side?

____

____

Use that memory as confidence that next time that you'll make it through as well.

You Can't Drive on "E"

You may have heard something similar before: "You can't pour from an empty cup." Ever drive down the road almost outta gas and worried if you'd make it to the next gas station? To clarify, I don't do it often, but the closest I ever came to running out of gas was 1 mile until empty. I'll never forget my anxiety that day! I was on my way to work, running late, wasn't sure if I could make it and get gas right after close by or had to stop beforehand, and I missed my exit on the highway! Obviously, I should've been more preemptive and filled my tank the day before.

In life, you can't drive on "E" either. I see it all the time, especially in parents. We tend to give so much of our focus to our kids, chores, school, kids' activities, and working to provide for them that we lose sight of our own goals and dreams. I often hear, "I just don't have time for myself." Sound familiar? Yes, there are some pretty busy stages of life, especially as a parent. I'll touch more on this later. Again, we all have the same 24 hours in a day. It's not about having time, it's about prioritizing time better.

If you need to, start small: 5 min of yoga or squats and pushups in the morning, use Duolingo for 5-10 min a day to learn a new language, find a hobby both you and your kids enjoy that you can do together, go to the gym on your lunch break, start eating healthier so you have more energy, schedule a babysitter and date night, wake up 30 min before you kids for some quiet time or focus on it for 30 min before bed. Are these things going to be easy? Doubtful. Are they worth it, and even necessary? *Absolutely!*

Those who don't make time for themselves wind up bitter and broken. In life, we get *better* or *bitter*. Those are the only options. Parents often feel depressed, lost, and lonely once their kids move out. Part of that is because they didn't make time for themselves for 20 years and lost themselves once they became parents. It's also why many marriages end up unhappy after the kids move out. They didn't make time for each other, either; and they feel like they're living with a stranger now.

For those that don't have kids, if you give everything to your career, what will you have left for the life you wanted from the money from that career? We tend to give so much of our energy to a job we don't like that pays us too little, and can replace us tomorrow if we quit. I often hear, "Well, I can't stand the job or long hours, but it's job security." Guess what: there's no such thing as job security. If you own your own business, you know the struggle and hustle required to build it and keep it going. If you work for someone else, believe me regardless of how stable the company seems, it can still go under tomorrow. They aren't going to tell you until the day they let you go.

When I was a Personal Training Director, my wife and I started doing some nutrition coaching on the side. Not long after, we realized the potential. I quit my job and went back to part-time personal training. I worked for a company that had partnered with the same gyms for many years. Five months later, the two companies had a falling out, the gym broke contract, and the gym managers escorted every trainer off the premises across 24 locations within a couple of hours. Fortunately, we started a few gyms of our own really quickly. When I asked what would have happened had I still been a manager, they said they wouldn't have had a gym for me and I would've been let go.

There is no true job security. Remember that the next time you say "yes" to working an extra shift and having to sacrifice time for yourself, that trip you planned with friends, or your child's baseball game.

What are you currently doing that's fully for yourself?

____

____

What can you implement starting this week that's fully for you? Start small at first if needed.

____

____

Weather the Storms

How many times have you been on the road and had to deal with storms? We do our best to plan for them, drive slow, sometimes take another route, or occasionally have to delay a day or two. The same happens in life. Storms will always happen; and like real storms, we can't control them. They come in the form of unexpected break ups, layoffs, injuries, and sometimes real storms that can really impact our plans.

For some reason, there's this common expectation that when we decide to take action towards our goals and dreams, it'll be sunny, clear skies the whole time. Some think, "Well, of course there will be a little rain." *False!* There will sometimes be hurricanes and tornadoes! In fact, there will be countless storms along the way. We can try a different route, go slower, or delay our plans. With an actual storm, we can just go home or stay at a friend's house. When it comes to your dream life, just make sure you don't fully give up. You may have to go home with your tail tucked between your legs, but the sun will shine again and you *must* get back out there!

I was fired from two of my first jobs; injured my knee, shin, pec, and back in the past; went through some tough break ups, dealt with losses of loved ones and broken down cars, and countless other storms. None of it was easy, and oftentimes it was scary. None of it stopped me from chasing my dreams, though.

The same applies in your health journey. People often think it'll be sunshine and rainbows, or at least a lot easier than what it is. Even with the proper guidance, there will still be storms. You'll be crushing it in the gym, then get injured and be out for a while or have to dial things back. You'll be doing well with your nutrition, then get a stomach bug and be living off of soup for a week. You'll be on your way to the gym, and your kid's school calls letting you know he's sick and you have to come pick him up. You'll go grocery shopping, and your favorite healthy food is outta stock so you have to substitute.

I tell my clients: It doesn't get easier, you just get better. Storms WILL occur. Expect them, do your best to be ready for them, and endure them. Your dream life is still waiting for you on the other side.

What storms have you gone through in the past?

____

____

How are you preparing for future storms?

____

____

Bathroom Breaks

You can't have road trips without bathroom breaks. On the road to our dream lives, I view bathroom breaks as a quick pause and reset. On the road, we stop to use the bathroom, refuel the car, stretch our legs, adjust the GPS if needed, and grab some food and drinks as well.

In our life journey, this is a time to pause and reflect. We think about how far we've come, recheck how far we have to go to reach our goals, and take a moment to appreciate the road we've traveled so far. After a quick bathroom break, we feel more refreshed and ready to tackle the next leg of our road trip, correct?

Same goes in life. Sure, that quick break may seem to slow us down slightly, but if we do not take a moment to reset, we'll run outta gas. We'll get anxious, forget how far we've come, focus too much on how far we still have to go, and the journey won't be as enjoyable. We may even quit and turn around!

On the road I have no problem taking bathroom breaks, but in life I admit that I struggle with them. There's times when I have so many audacious goals and have a hard time pausing for a moment to be grateful for how far I've come. We've all heard about having an attitude of gratitude. I can't stress how important it is. In the times where I do well with it and focus on daily gratitude, it definitely helps me stay fueled up and energized to keep heading down the road to my dreams.

The small wins are part of the journey to the big wins, and those small wins include the obstacles you've made it through. You've already come so far in your journey. Do not take that for granted. Use the memories of what you've overcome to remind you of how strong you are. Make sure that you're taking bathroom breaks to reflect and reset. You've overcome everything so far in life, or you wouldn't be reading this right now. That's a 100% success rate! I'd say those are pretty good odds.

I may not do well with gratitude sometimes, but something that's helped me a lot is the time to reflect and reset. A big part of how I do this is by reading personal development books. I think about where my biggest weaknesses are, then I research a book about that topic and read it. It sounds simple enough, yet it's had a dramatic impact on my life the past five years. People often say knowledge is power, but I never fully understood that until I started reading these books. That's the point of *this* book. I want this book to be part of your bathroom break to reflect and reset.

Pause right now. What have you overcome on your journey that you can be grateful for?

____

____

What's a weakness you know you have?

____

____

If you feel this book has already helped you, look up a book about that weakness you just wrote and order it now. It'll be the next book you read.

____

____

Hills

On the road, when you're driving up hills, you have to press harder on the gas pedal. You can feel it being harder on the car and using more gas to make it. In life, it's no different. It seems like it would be nice if the road to our dream life were a straight shot without any hills. Honestly, it wouldn't mean as much if we didn't overcome some hills along the way to reach our goals. It can be hard staying on your health journey, eating right, going to the gym, and going to bed on time then not hitting snooze in the morning. It can be hard continuing to apply for jobs in your dream field of choice, especially after rejecttion. It can be hard studying for test after test in school.

The good news is that there are downhills too! On the road, once we overcome the hills, we get to enjoy the other side where we can take our foot off the gas a little for a short time. It's the fun part and you can feel it being easier on the car as well.

In life, we can look forward to coasting downhill. There's times when it's easier, where all our hard work has paid off, where we have more fun, and it feels like things are finally coming together. We crush new health goals, our new routines seem easier to follow, we find that dream job, and we crush all our finals. It can be such a stress reliever, and we may wanna sit back and relax. This can also be where we really mess up; and if we aren't careful, we won't be ready for the next uphill battle.

What do we have to do on the downhills of life that often gets overlooked? When you're on the road, can you take your hands off the steering wheel? Definitely not, or you'll run off the road. If you keep your foot off the gas for too long, will you make it up the next uphill? No way, unless it's really small and even then you'll be moving pretty slow at the top!

Even in the seemingly easier parts of life where everything is coming together, we have to keep up the habits that got us there in the first place. We have to keep our eyes on the road and prepare for the next uphill battle, because *believe me* there WILL be more. In fact, if we use the downhill properly, we can use the momentum to make the next uphill a little easier!

So, how do we keep the momentum going in life? I mentioned earlier the book *The Slight Edge* by Jeff Olson, wand he talks about this. It's keeping up the habits that got you over the hill in the first place. If we totally relax on the downhill and stop doing what got us to the top, we'll wind up stuck at the bottom. Success leaves clues. When you get over that hill, review what got you there and learn how to keep it going.

Remember, there will ALWAYS be more uphill battles in life, and it's the downhill portions that help us get from one to the next. If the road were always flat, it would actually be quite boring. We can't have the downhills without the uphills. They're both equally important. Welcome them both.

What uphill battles are you trying to climb right now?

____

____

What downhill rides are you looking forward to that will help you keep climbing?

____

____

What habits are you keeping up on the downhill to keep your eyes on the road, hands on the steering wheel, and foot ready to hit the gas?

____

____

Road Rage

Those words alone probably bring back memories of someone flipping you off or screaming at you from their car, then cutting you off and possibly almost running you off the road. We've all had to deal with it at some point. Perhaps it's something you've dealt with on the other side as well, having a hard time controlling your emotions and getting irate with someone on the road.

There's definitely road rage in life, too! Someone accuses us of stealing their job or potential significant other. We make a mistake (like forgetting to use a blinker or not seeing someone in our blind spot), and it causes someone more work or messes up their plans for the day or week. We get a report turned in late at school or work, and our boss or teacher gets upset. We forget our anniversary, and our spouse makes us sleep on the couch. All of these examples can happen with us on the other side as well, and really get on our nerves.

Here's the hard truth: We ALL make mistakes, and they often derail our plans or someone else's plans. Can we stop all mistakes from happening? Definitely not! If we could, there wouldn't be mistakes. So what can we do? Sure, we can learn from them to try and do better next time, but for the ones that still happen, we can still control one thing: Our *response!* I'm not saying it's easy. It takes WORK, and a lot of it, to learn how to navigate and control our emotions better. If it were easy, there wouldn't b management meetings.

Believe me, it's worth the effort. Think of how dangerou can be if you have road rage on the road, or someone el does towards you. It can very likely cause an accident. I someone else flips us off and cuts us off, turning it into a race and trying to get around them will only make the situation worse.

The same is true in life. We've all heard, "An eye for an eye makes the whole world blind." Of course, we don't want to continue to get run over; and if someone keeps doing it, then yes, we have to address the situation and find a way to put a stop to it. This could mean sitting down and having a conversation with the person (or a boss if it's at work), or possibly finding a way to no longer interact with that person anymore if they won't change.

Remember, all we can control is our own thoughts and actions, and only in the present. Move on from the road rage of others, focus on your own goals, and learn how to navigate the stresses so that you do not cause road rage yourself. This may be through yoga, meditation, prayer, pausing to breathe, going to therapy, listening to podcasts, or reading books.

Here's a super simple one to keep your cool: when someone frustrates you, before you respond (whether it's in person or through text, or on a call, and *especially* if it's video), take a big drink of water. It gives an obvious reason for you to pause, and allows you a few seconds to collect your thoughts and reply more logically than emotionally.

For me personally, the immediate solution is taking a breath and taking a drink of water. Aside from that, I also use my workouts to let off steam as well as martial arts. I've never used my martial arts abilities on someone with the intent to harm them. A big reason for that is focusing on other ways to deal with the stress and frustration.

I've had countless frustrating situations over the years since I first started training in martial arts over 14 years ago, and I could've used it as a solution, but it never would've actually been a solution. It would've only made things worse. I've used my words when I can, and removed myself from the situation when words didn't work. Instead, I use it for training in case a situation ever arises where I need to protect myself or my loved ones, and words and removing myself from the situation aren't working. It can be very therapeutic!

Wailing on a bag rather than a person or someone's property can get out a lot of aggression in a much healthier way, though I'd recommend making sure you have at least somewhat of a handle on your road rage in life before starting in case that rage gets the best of you and you do something you'll regret.

Back to the exercise part: Exercise releases endorphins which helps reduce stress. I always feel better and calmer after a great workout. If you struggle with road rage yourself, perhaps a morning workout before you go to work will help! If it's a boss or coworker that's always angry and causing issues, perhaps getting in a workout on your lunch break to get away (or right after work) can help alleviate that stress before you get home to your family.

It will likely take some trial and error to find what works for you. I also recommend reading books and listening to podcasts that can help. The important thing is to keep trying. Causing road rage or having to deal with road rage all the time isn't good for anyone.

What, or who, is causing road rage in your life currently?

____

____

How can you navigate it better or remove it entirely from your path?

____

____

What road rage are you perhaps causing in life that you need to let go?

____

____

What can you do differently moving forward?

____

____

Terrain

It can feel amazing flying down a smooth expressway that's well kept. Unfortunately, that's not all we drive on, and that's definitely not all we get in life, either. Sometimes, we have to drive rockier roads. For instance, I grew up on a gravel road. Until I was 20 years old, I had to deal with the dust, flying rocks, cars that were always dirty, and the occasional dings and windshield cracks. You also can't (or shouldn't, at least) drive too fast on a gravel road.

In life, we get rough terrain sometimes as well. We may still feel like we're on the right path to our dreams, but things just seem slower. Gravel roads in life are rocky, uneasy, and we proceed with caution. We're more uncertain than normal of what lies ahead, whether we're nervous about joining a gym, worried we won't do well in interviews, or scared about that first date. We feel we're making the right decisions, but it's still scary.

I definitely felt like I was on a gravel road when I transitioned into personal training. I was leaving a full-time salaried IT job in a promising career field for a commission-based industry where my success and pay each month were solely up to me. I had to work my tail off, and worked both jobs for a while before I built up enough of a personal training business that I could leave that IT job. There's definitely been a lot of ups and downs over the years between switching gyms and companies and having to completely rebuild my business numerous times. But, I'm so glad I made the leap! While it's been rocky for sure, I'm so much happier in the fitness industry, I've learned FAR more than I ever did in IT, I make more money than I did in that job, I control my own schedule, and I've never been more fulfilled!

Also, just like I got used to that gravel road I grew up on, the fitness industry road feels a lot smoother for me now, too. Each new road in life will likely feel a little rocky at first. Hang in there, take your time, and keep going! It'll get smoother, or at least feel like it over time.

Then, there's the roads we all dread: Those covered in snow and ice. I lived the first 35 years of my life in Missouri (before moving to sunny Florida), and we dealt with horrible road conditions every winter. The temperature is so all over the place that it could be 75° one day and 30° the next. When it snowed, oftentimes it would melt, then refreeze, which made for some terrifying driving experiences. I've had numerous accidents over the years, and I can't even put a number on the amount of times I didn't know if I'd make it to where I was going.

This brings us to how this applies to the road to our dream life. Icy roads are when we feel like we've had total loss of control. We know the path we need to take, yet we're completely unsure if we're going to make it. I've been there so many times myself. Our relationship isn't going well; everytime we get paid, another bill pops up we didn't expect; we feel we could be laid off at any moment, and it just feels like nothing is set in stone. Sound familiar? To be honest, we felt some of this with moving to Florida. We love SO much about Florida, but we weren't prepared for how expensive it can be. Our first year was pretty rough, and we didn't know if we were going to make it. We persevered, and eventually it got better. We buckled down on expenses, and focused on expanding our careers.

It also helped that we built some amazing friendships with people that supported and encouraged us throughout. If you do not have those, get them immediately. We actually met our closest friends through Facebook (Meta) groups. There's times when we may wanna give up, turn around, and go back to what's comfortable.

I remember a time when I did just that. I worked at Office Max (now Office Depot), and on my way to work the roads were so bad that I actually fish tailed and hit the guardrail on the highway. I called work and told them I wasn't making it in, then went home. They were mad, but I wasn't taking the risk. That one day of work isn't that big of a deal compared to risking my life. I still went to work the next day, though!

On the road to our dream life, we may have delays due to terrain, but we need to keep trucking along to get to our destination. We still have to weigh the risks, but believe me, many of the risks are worth it. Your dream destination is there waiting for you. I'm definitely glad we didn't give up on Florida.

There WILL be rocky and icy roads on the path to your dream life. Accept them, navigate them the best you can, and keep moving forward. The worst feeling is allowing them to make you turn around, and never find out what's possible for you. Believe me, if you do not, you'll always wonder what was at the end of that tough terrain.

What gravel roads are you on right now in life?

____

____

What are you doing to navigate them?

____

____

What snowy/icy roads are you on right now in life?

____

____

How are you navigating them? Who are you talking to about them that will help support and encourage you?

____

____

Kids in the Back Seat

I know that I touched on this before, but it's worth discussing more. If you're a parent, you probably just heard screaming and crying in your head. Hopefully, you thought of some fun and cute times too, though! Whether it's getting them in and out of the car, stopping for bathroom breaks, getting onto them for fighting or throwing things at each other (or you), or answering them for the 100th time if we're there yet, kids can definitely make any road trip more challenging. The same goes for the road to our dream life.

Between diapers, school, extracurricular activities, play dates, getting them to bed, getting them up in the morning, getting them to eat their food, and all the other chaotic times, it can seem like we no longer have time for our own goals and dreams. I'd say it's very common that parents give up their own goals aside from maybe career advancement once they have kids. I totally understand it. It's not easy to keep fighting for your dreams in those chaotic 20 years or so of raising a child.

Here's the thing…You have to do it anyway. If you do not, you're giving away some of your best years, then waiting til you're retired, broke, and broken from decades of not making any time for yourself. We have two young boys at the time that I'm writing this, and even between school, diapers, and everything else, I'm still making time to write this book. I'm studying Spanish and focusing on my nutrition and exercise as well. Though I'm not currently, I've also made time for kenpo. If you do not make time for yourself, you'll lose yourself. That's why so many parents feel lost when their kids become adults and move out.

Here's another way to think about it: I often hear some version of, "Now that I have kids, they deserve all the attention. It's my job to focus everything on them. It's a sacrifice I made when I decided to have kids." If that's what you believe, I have a question for you. When your kids grow up and have kids of their own, do you want their lives to essentially be over as well, or do you want them to continue to have goals and dreams of their own? If you give everything to your kids, you'll have nothing left when they move out; and, you're teaching them to do the same thing. I don't know about you, but I want my kids fighting for their dream lives their WHOLE lives.

Also remember this: Your ceiling will be your kids' floor. They'll likely base their potential on you. Of course, you're going to encourage them to chase their dreams; but, if they do not see you doing the same, they'll assume that when they have kids, then they'll have to give up, too. Tell them constantly how much you believe in them, AND chase your own dreams in the process. You'll both likely learn a lot along the way, and you'll set your kids up for even greater success. Kids do not always listen to what we say, but they watch what we do. What are you showing them?

Now, all of this said, I'm not saying to ignore your kids. Quite the opposite! Ironically, even though I see most parents aren't traveling the road to their dream lives, they aren't spending enough quality time with their kids, either! Technology has changed things greatly. Being in the same room and everyone being on phones and tablets is *not* quality time. Staring at a TV and not communicating is *not* quality time. Do not just focus on more time together, focus on QUALITY time together.

Put the devices away, communicate with your kids, listen to them, try to understand them, make sure they feel heard, learn all their interests (even if those interests annoy you), learn about their own goals and dreams, then encourage and support the heck out of them! Be there through all of their wins and losses, successes and struggles, times of joy and times of sadness.

Now, where do you find time for yourself? I understand that when they're young, it can be really tough. They want all of your attention, and they do not understand that you need time as well. Just like in a car, they constantly want you to look at stuff, or ask questions, while you're trying to pay attention to the road, or listen to the GPS, or your favorite song. Somehow, you still have to make time for those things though, correct? Otherwise, you'll run off the road or wind up somewhere you didn't intend to be! When they're young, we typically have to squeeze in time for ourselves in the nooks and crannies of our days. For example, I'm writing this book early in the morning each day before the kids wake up.

As they get older, it can get a little easier in some ways. Our oldest, who will be eight in a few days as I write this, is beginning to understand more that mommy and daddy need their time, too. He's more likely to keep quiet if we're trying to focus on the road or listen to the GPS. He'll let us listen to our favorite song because we do the same for him. If he wakes up before I'm done writing for the day, he'll let me focus on it because he knows we'll still have quality time together.

He sees that we're still fighting for our dream lives, and we see the wheels turning in his own mind. He talks about his goals and dreams in life, and though at his age they change often, we encourage him every time! Give your kids quality time, support their goals, and they'll do the same for you! This way, you're also teaching them that once they have kids someday, they can still continue on the road to their dream lives.

What areas of your personal goals have you given up on or slacked off on since having kids?

____

____

What can you do for even 10-15 min per day to get back to those goals and hobbies?

____

____

How much QUALITY time are you spending with your kids per day or week?

____

____

What are THEIR goals and dreams for their lives? If you can’t answer, it’s ok, just ask them today.

____

____

Gas Mileage

Fuel Efficiency

The more fuel efficient your vehicle is, the better gas mileage you get, correct? Same applies in life. Gas is your motivation. It comes and goes. Some days you have it, and some days you do not. People often think they have to wait until they have more motivation, or blame their lack of motivation, as to why they can't get anything done. To a degree, I understand. Ever try to drive without much gas in your tank? You're not getting far. Earlier, we discussed how making time for yourself helps fill your tank. How do we keep it there, though?

This is where gas mileage comes into play. It's determined by your habits, both good and bad. Habits that are moving you closer to your goals are like highway driving. Poor habits are like city driving or driving erratically. There's days when we all lack motivation, and days when we feel like we can conquer the world. Especially on the days where motivation is non-existent, we *mus*t and will *always* rely on our habits. Some are simple, like brushing our teeth or showering. Things we've done our whole lives can be a lot easier to keep up, and we do not even realize they're considered habits. Going to the gym, meal prepping, setting a specific sleep schedule, or taking up a new hobby can be more challenging.

Remember, we have to start small. Your first workout may be 10 squats and pushups right when you get outta bed. Your first meal prepping may be just grilling some chicken and adding in some steam bags of veggies. You may set an alarm to go to bed on time, then make sure your alarm clock or phone isn't near the bed so that you have to get up to stop it. If your new hobby is learning a new language, it may start with five minutes per day as soon as you get up or right before you go to bed.

Now let's look at the other side of habits, the ones that are destroying our gas mileage. Staying up late instead of going to bed on time, sitting all the time at home instead of standing when possible, ordering pizza twice a week rather than cooking, or playing games on your phone rather than getting that new language lesson done or working that side hustle. Believe me, I've been guilty of all of these at one time or another. The time will pass regardless. You can look back being proud of what you've accomplished with good habits, or look back at all the bad ones and feel guilty for not fixing it sooner. The good news is that you can change your habits starting today!

Adjusting our habits can seem small at first, but it can have a profound impact on our gas mileage over time. With the proper habits in place (and you'll likely have to tweak them many times to determine what works best for you), it can make things drastically easier to stay on track. Yes, sometimes discipline is needed, but overall it comes down to habits.

Even if you floor it occasionally, thinking "Oh, I'm way behind! I'll just get it all done today," keeping that mentality will only result in more stress. Sooner or later, that won't work. It will still be a lot harder to reach your goals and dreams. If you work on your habits and create consistency, then even on the days you don't really want to, you'll do the things that you know you need to do.

Out of Gas and Pushing the Car

Ever had to push a car before? I have, and it's rough! I've done it numerous times, actually. Some were because the car totally broke down, and we had to get it home (if we were close) or at least off the road. Some pushes were to help get the car started. In life, your gas mileage may be amazing, you may have all the great habits in place; and sometimes, you still may feel like you're pushing the car uphill to get it started.

In these situations, people often say they lack discipline. Believe me, I feel the same way at times. So, how do I overcome that feeling? How do I do it anyway? I think about where either option will lead me. How will I feel later that day if I push the car? How will I feel if I don't? If I push the car, I'll feel accomplished. If I don't, I'll probably regret it later.

Sure, sometimes I think of the long term impact of continually doing the thing or not doing the thing, but in the moment, that often doesn't help me much. I have to focus on the immediate impact both physically and mentally. In fact, that's human nature. We're wired with a survival instinct to go for the instant gratification over the long term benefit. This is why we need to focus on the short term benefits of our habits as well.

Here are a couple examples: For quite some time, I worked out at 5:30 in the morning (currently, I workout midday). It was NEVER easy. I almost always felt like a zombie walking into the gym, and even the warm up sets were tough as my body loosened up. Yet, EVERY time I walked outta the gym, I felt more energized, grateful, and ready to tackle the day (not to mention the feeling of accomplishment all day knowing that I got up early and got it done).

How did I get out of bed early, though? I thought about that "after" feeling, and how I'd feel the rest of the day BEFORE I ever went to the gym. I imagined how great I was going to feel, and on the flip side, I thought about how much I'd regret it and be mad at myself later if I didn't get it done.

Now, think about that feeling after getting an oil change that's long overdue, or filling up your gas tank when you weren't sure if you were even going to make it to the gas station. There's a sense of relief and almost accomplishment, right?

Putting in the work to take care of the only vehicle you'll ever have in life (yourself and your body) creates an immediate sense of accomplishment that you can focus on to keep going. We live in an instant gratification world, and it almost always wins over the long term benefits. The long term may get you started, but the immediate can help keep you going.

If you want to learn more about habits, check out *Atomic Habits by James Clear* and *High Performance Habits by Brendon Burchard*, two of my favorite books.

What habits do you currently have that improve your gas mileage?

____

____

What habits in your life are messing it up?

____

____

What habit adjustment can you make starting today that will improve your gas mileage? Remember, keep it small at first.

____

____

What do you think helps you when you have to push the car?

____

____

Vehicle Health

If your car is leaking oil, has really low gas mileage, a flat tire, worn out brake pads, or a transmission that's on the fritz, it's not going to go very far, correct? Well, the same goes for your body. When it comes to actual vehicles, if push comes to shove, you can always get a new one. We may be able to replace some parts in our vehicle for life, but we can't just get a new body. We've all known people who don't take care of their vehicles, and unfortunately the number of people that don't take care of themselves is far greater.

Getting oil changes, making sure you don't completely run outta gas, getting your tires realigned, replacing or cleaning your air filter, and getting general tune ups are all investments in your car. Just like you want the right gas and oil in your vehicle for it to run optimally, you also need to fuel your body with the right food to help it run optimally as well. Remember, every cell in your body comes from your food. You are *literally* what you eat. What are you made of?

Ever drive a car after it's been sitting for a while, and it sounds or feels rough? We also have to exercise on a regular basis to keep our bodies from getting stiff and feeling rough. After age 30, we lose roughly 1% lean muscle mass per YEAR if we aren't working on it! Between the ages of 40 and 80, we lose about 30-50% of our lean muscle mass. It's why we see elderly people break bones more often and not eat as much. Exercise strengthens your bones, and having muscle supports them. For every pound of muscle you have, you burn roughly another 100 calories per day, so your metabolism is higher too.

Anyone can exercise, it just may look a little different if you already have limitations. I've worked with people over the years who are blind, wearing a boot on their leg, had multiple knee replacements, several back surgeries and fusions, countless shoulder issues, and so many other limitations. Make sure you find a certified professional to help guide you, and together you can build that strength and metabolism back.

Let's also discuss drinking water. Water is the oil for your body. Drinking more water can help alleviate joint pain, aids digestion, flushes out toxins, helps with sleep and energy, and actually helps you feel full longer. The bare minimum is 64 oz per day, though I recommend at least 100 oz, especially if you're exercising. Often, when you're hungry, drink water first. Your body may just be thirsty, and it doesn't always know the difference. If you do not drink enough water, your body will recycle dirty water. Think about that the next time you slack on drinking water. Recycled water? That's just nasty.

Car Repairs

If we drive a car long enough, there's bound to be car repairs needed. It could be anything from a flat tire to replacing the entire transmission. Taking good care of our vehicle definitely helps, but things will still happen. You can't predict hitting a nail on the road, or someone rear ending you.

When it comes to our bodies, taking care of it can greatly reduce the risk of heart disease, diabetes, high cholesterol, high blood pressure, and even cancer; but, things can still happen. We've all gotten the flu or a cold at some point, most of us have had an injury or some type of surgery, and we may be predisposed to certain diseases that we are unaware of.

This is one of the reasons, just like getting your car checked out to avoid unseen issues getting worse, that it's important to get regular checkups, bloodwork, and even genetic testing for ourselves as well. Chris Hemsworth, who played Thor (and everyone knows as super fit), discovered through testing that he's at high risk of developing Alzheimer's when he's older, so he's taking action to help prevent it as much as he can.

Regardless of what we do, some things will still happen. This doesn't mean to just sit back and do nothing, but be ready for it as best you can. We can't have a backup body like a car, or even go rent one, but we can have certain things in place. Making sure we have good health insurance is a big one, having close friends or family that you know can help out with things temporarily, making sure you have a few extra days of PTO outside of vacations (btw, vacations are part of self care), and having some extra money in savings in case you miss more work than your PTO allows.

Circling back to building muscle, building muscle helps you overcome injuries better, too. Again, your muscles help support your bones. The more lean muscle you have, the easier it is for you to navigate injuries and still be able to get around. I had a stress fracture many years ago in my leg, and I didn't get around nearly as well as I have since then with other injuries and surgeries because I didn't lift weights back then. Since then, I've had a hernia, abscess, knee injury, nearly tore my pec, and tweaked my back numerous times. Each time has been tough, but I focused on what I could control; and, I know I got around easier because I lift weights and eat pretty healthy on a regular basis. Yes, some of those injuries were from exercising, but I think of all the situations where I nearly had an injury but didn't because I workout all the time.

Your body is the vehicle to take you to your dream life. Do you want to drive a Lamborghini, or a Ford Fiesta? Btw, I had a Ford Fiesta. It died the month of my last payment when the transmission went out…

What are you doing currently to eat better?

____

____

What changes can you make starting today to improve it?

____

____

What type of exercises are you currently engaged in and how often?

____

____

What changes can you make starting today to improve it?

____

____

How much actual water are you drinking per day on average?

____

____

What changes can you make starting today to improve it?

____

____

What repairs have you dealt with in the past?

____

____

How did you navigate them? How are you still navigating them?

____

____

How are you prepared for future repairs?

____

____

Rear View Mirror

You may have heard before there's a reason the rear view mirror is so small and the windshield is so big. We need to focus more on what's ahead than what's behind us. I want to take some time to add to that, and there's an area that's left out.

First, let's talk about that mirror. I often hear people constantly reminiscing about the past, talking about how great things used to be, and wishing things would go back to the way they were. I also see people sharing so many memories on Facebook (Meta), yet you never see any new adventures from them.

Yes, we wanna look in the mirror sometimes, it's there for a reason. If you stare at it all the time, though, you'll lose sight of and control of what's happening in front of you. You can still have plenty of new adventures and reach plenty of new goals; but first, you have to take your eyes off the rear view mirror way more often. That doesn't mean we don't look at it sometimes. It's good to remember the good times, be grateful for what you've overcome, and learn from the past to make the future better.

I often remind myself of the schooling I've gone through, the books I've read, the podcasts I've listened to, the weight I've lifted in the gym, the adventures I've had, and the 4th degree black belt I've earned. I'll also never forget the loneliness I felt as a kid on the playground, the bullying I received, the invisibility I felt, and the self doubt and lack of self esteem I'm constantly fighting. I do not dwell on the good or the bad. I'll never forget any of it, but I focus a lot more on what's ahead of me, all I want to accomplish, and the people I want to help overcome the struggles I've been through, just like many have been there for me.

Now, let's talk about the part that phrase leaves out. If the rear view mirror is the past and what's outside your windshield is the future, what about the present? That's what/who's in the car with you. On the road to your dream life, you'll have a lot of people alongside you at different times. It's important to live in the moment with those you care about and who support you. It's important to truly focus on and enjoy the adventures you're currently experiencing. Embrace the things you're learning. Be grateful for the people and things in your life right now.

Yes, you need to look in the rear view mirror sometimes; and, of course, much of your time is looking ahead and planning for what's coming up. Just do not forget what's in the car with you is likely a huge part of what's driving you to chase your dreams anyway.

Part of the point of a road trip is the journey. If your only focus is reaching your destination, it's probably going to be pretty boring or cause you a lot of stress. You're constantly looking at the ETA, cutting bathroom breaks as short as you can, and ignoring the sites along the way. Your family would be pretty bored, as well; and, there would likely be more fights in the car. Taking the time to enjoy the journey makes it more fun, and you'll create even more great memories to look back on in that rear view mirror.

My family and I have a lot of goals and dreams ahead of us. We've accomplished a lot together, and we're far from finished. We discuss what we want to happen often, and try our best to put it into action; but, we also spend time living in the moment. We make sure we create new adventures, from going to Disney or the beach to just watching a movie together or playing a game.

In fact, here's a parenting hack for you: If you truly take time to sometimes let go of the past and future, live in the moment with your kids, and create quality memories, they age slower. Parents often get so sad when their kids get older, and a big part of that is because they spent too much time focused on the past and future that they've lost sight of the present. Do not miss what's in the car with you. Plan for the future, learn from the past, do not skip the present, and be grateful for the journey.

What in the past are you too focused on that you need to let go of, at least a little?

____

____

What in the present are you currently overlooking that you need to spend more intentional time on?

____

____

Car Lights

Turn Signal

One of my biggest pet peeves is when people on the road do not use their turn signal. If you're going to get over in my lane, I want to know ahead of time so that we do not collide and I do not have to slam on the breaks. It's important to let others know what you're going to do next.

In life, the turn signal means sharing your journey publicly. Some believe it's best to keep everything to yourself and grow in the dark. Flowers need sunlight to grow, right? Even though I hate dieting, we often say don't diet in the dark. When you're on the road to your dream life, the more people that know you're making moves, the better. They do not need to know every detail, but letting others in not only gives them a chance to support you, but it also increases your accountability.

I don't know about you, but if I accidentally turn my turn signal on, I'll typically get over just so I don't look dumb. Even while writing this book, I've shared numerous times how far I've come on social media for that extra accountability. Especially nowadays, with social media you never know who may actually be able to help you. If you're looking for a specific job, you may actually know someone that's hiring for it that you didn't realize. If you're working on your health (which I hope you're at least thinking about by now), you may know a health coach or personal trainer that can help. If not, contact me and I can help with that, too. If you're wanting to learn martial arts, or a new instrument, or a language, you may know someone that can help in those areas as well. Even if you're looking for a significant other, putting that out there may even help you find that person!

I'm constantly posting about my health journey, not just because I'm in the industry and want to help others, but also because, even for me, it's extra accountability so that I stay on track better. I also post about dad wins and struggles, life goals, etc. I'm a pretty open book, and because of that, I've had a lot of help over the years from people that I never expected. These are the people who slow down or switch lanes themselves to get outta the way when you've got your turn signal on.

Here's a perfect example. As I write this, yesterday was day one of a caffeine detox that I started for a couple weeks (at least) because I realized that my caffeine intake had gotten way out of hand lately. I need a reset. Yesterday morning at the gym, I mentioned to one of my clients that I'm doing it, and he told me he struggles with it, too. In fact, because I shared it with him and told him it was day one for me, he decided he's going to do the same! Yesterday evening and this morning, I admit that I was tempted to cave; but, I thought of him, and I didn't. If it weren't for sharing that with him, I don't know if I would've endured. We all need accountability partners in life sometimes!

Side note of this: If you find an accountability partner and they bail on you (which is likely to happen), then find another one. Here's another example: When I was 23, my cousin, who I love dearly, talked me into signing up for a marathon (26.2 miles). I had never ran more than three miles, and she had never ran more than 5, so I convinced her to do a half marathon instead (13.1 miles). She agreed, then I looked up how to train for it (this was long before I went back to school for personal training), and started running. A couple months in, I asked how her training was going. She hadn't even started, and decided that she wasn't going to run it. I wasn't mad at all, I understood, but I needed a new accountability partner. I talked to my coworkers, and two of the women that I worked with at the time actually signed up and ran it, too! They followed a different training program than I did, and we didn't run it side by side, but we still talked about it regularly throughout our training (and after the run, as well). It really helped!

Let's talk for a moment about the other side of what happens when we share with others. Sometimes, when you turn your turn signal on, someone will speed up to be even more in your way. These people exist on the road to your dream life as well. Not everyone will be supportive and putting your goals and dreams out there will give them an opportunity to be jerks. It's part of the process. At least, now, you know who to disconnect from and block on social media. Remember, it's ok for people to disagree. It's NOT ok for them to be disrespectful. If you want to try to talk to them, go ahead; but if you can't resolve the issue, move on and leave them in the dust. Do not let the negative people deter you from sharing, or you'll never find those amazing supportive people that you may not have even met yet.

Now, what happens if you decide to never share with others? If you do not use your turn signal, you're more likely to cause an accident on the road, which will delay you or keep you from your destination. If you do not share your goals and dreams with anyone else out of fear they'll say mean things or try to steal your ideas, what's more likely to happen is that you'll just quit or procrastinate.

Believe me, I've seen it for years in the fitness industry. Those that do not share their health goals with others are far more likely to just give up on them, because no one knows they're a quitter if they never knew they started. I'm assuming that you've thought about your dream life for a long time, and you do not want to be a quitter. Share it loud and proud. If you do not share, and then quit, sure, no one else will know, but *you* still will.

If you do not want to share on social media, that's ok, but make sure you're sharing regularly with others.

Who do you tell/will you tell (minimum two people) about your goals and dreams to increase your accountability?

____

____

If you're open to sharing your goals and dreams on social media (and haven't yet or haven't in a while), then write here what you will post about and do it today. In fact, do it as soon as you stop reading today.

____

____

Brake Lights

Brake lights exist to let others know that you're slowing down quickly, correct? It's not only important to share with others the goals and dreams you're going for, it's important to share when you need to take a minute, too. Sometimes, we have to take a short break. Other things pop up in our lives, and we need to take a moment to recalibrate. That doesn't mean that you come to a full stop and sit on the side of the road for five years, just slow down.

Sharing that you need to take a break allows those that care about you to support you even more, be there to lean on and to listen, and even help out physically with things you may need, or give advice on how you can get back up to speed. It's OK to share your struggles with others. In fact, if you want to inspire others along the way, this is a great way to do it. Nowadays, people are so filtered on social media, that sharing when you need a minute can connect you with others more. You may even find your next best passenger that will help guide you, or be each other's accountability partners (as they may be going through the same thing and feel alone until you share your side).

If you know enough to set a time frame on how long you need to slow down, then sharing that will also increase your own accountability when it's time to speed back up. Only sharing the highlights of our journey will get us stuck when things don't go as well; and if we aren't careful, we may end up feeling more alone than ever. We all know we aren't perfect, and trying to make others think we are will cause us to lose the passengers we need, or at least not give them the opportunity to help us when we need it. Use the brake lights when you need to. Let others know about your tough roads.

In what areas of your life are you currently hitting the brakes?

____

____

Who are you sharing it with?

____

____

Emergency Lights

Normally, when things go wrong, we just have to hit the brakes; but sometimes, it's much worse than that. We need the emergency lights. We have to stop, and we need help. On the road, we use our emergency lights to signal that we're in distress, so that someone can come help us (or just so others know we're working on fixing it ourselves so they don't hit us).

In life, emergency lights are important when you feel like there's no way you're going to get out of the situation you're in. It's OK to ask for help. At the very least, tell others about the heavy things that are happening in your life so that they can support you, even if you do not need actual help. These situations can take up all your thoughts, make you feel powerless, and (if you aren't careful) cause you to lose hope that you'll ever reach your dream destination. I've been in these situations many times. Believe me, hang in there. It may not seem like it at the time, but things *will* get better.

Do not beat yourself up over these situations, either. We can't change the past, all we can do is adapt and move forward. Sometimes there's something we can learn from these emergencies to help avoid them in the future, and sometimes there isn't. Learn what you can, get help if you need it, then get back on the road.

When I was about 12 years old, I remember walking out on the playground feeling totally alone, even with friends there. Though I had *some* friends, I never felt I had a *best* friend, and it always seemed like I was picked last for everything. I sometimes cried myself to sleep at night over it. What did I do about it? Nothing! I never told a soul until I was an adult. If I could go back in time, I'd tell that 12 year old boy that he needs to talk to someone. Talk to his friends, parents, other family members, a counselor, *somebody*. I guarantee I would've saved myself a lot of heartache if I had just opened up about it. Do not sit on the side of the road without your emergency lights on if you need help. People will just think you're parked and drive right by.

What emergencies are you going through in life right now that you need to share with someone?

____

____

Who will you share it with TODAY?

____

____

Whether you're just changing lanes, needing to brake, or have an emergency, sharing it with others will not only let them know how they may be able to help and support you, but it can also do something else extraordinary! You may inspire them too!

Most people nowadays aren't really focused on the road to their dream life for various reasons. Using your turn signal to make adjustments shows them the road won't be a straight line, and that's ok. Using your brakes shows them they can't floor it all the time, and that it's ok to slow down sometimes. Using your emergency lights and then getting back on the road shows them emergencies will happen, and they can overcome them, too. If the ones you inspire are your loved ones, it also shows them they can ask for help, and you may be able to return the favor!

Packing

When we're getting ready for a road trip, we have to pack everything we need for it. To a certain degree, the same applies to our goals in life. We have to prepare for them. If you're going to apply for jobs, then you need to create or update your resume. If you're looking for a significant other, you may want to do some self care first, join dating sites or apps, or figure out where you want to meet people. If you're working on a new hobby, you may need to get equipment or supplies. If you're wanting to improve your health, you may want to research local gyms, recipes, nutrition, or exercise programs.

Preparation is important, but there's another important part of this. When you're packing for a road trip, if you're anything like my family and I, you're bound to forget something. It's frustrating, but you'll typically still get by without it.

On the road to your dream life, it's even harder to be fully prepared. You may have a decent picture of the end goal, yet you can't possibly be prepared for everything on the path before you. That's ok. Remember, imperfect action trumps perfect inaction. Waiting for the perfect time is the ultimate excuse to push off our dreams. Work with what you have, and get into action. The cool part is if you're on the way and forgot to prepare for something, you don't have to go back home like on a regular road trip. You simply learn, adapt, and move on. The hardest step is the first one. Stop trying to pack the car perfectly, and just get on the road.

If you just get started even though you aren't fully prepared, then you're still ahead of everyone else still sitting in their driveway. One of the greatest parts of imperfect action over perfect inaction is that while you know you will have to make some adjustments, you're building momentum, and that's *huge*!

Like I've mentioned before, I've switched jobs and careers many times in my life until I found my passion in health and fitness. There's no way I would've known that it was my passion and calling back when I first went to college for IT; but, I had to go down that path to determine it wasn't the right one. Throughout, I still learned a lot, and even still apply some skills today.

For instance, I've created tracking documents for clients which have been utilized in numerous other gyms. I've helped managers with shortcuts and workarounds to make their jobs easier, and being more organized has allowed me to impact a lot more lives. When I first started as a personal trainer, I still had a lot to learn. My training wasn't terrible, but it was lacking in many ways; and sometimes, there's things that you can only learn with experience. I've passed that information on as much as I can. I often tell people to learn from my mistakes, so that you do not have to make the same ones.

Before IT and fitness, I worked a ton of other jobs as well. While many of them were vastly different, like McDonald's and Office Max (now Office Depot), I learned things from all of them that still help me today. All of those tools and skills are packed in my car and ready for me to use when I need them.

Start working on that book today. You may just write a lot more than you think; but at the very least, ideas will come to you as you write like they have for me.

Start doing some form of exercise today. It may not be perfectly programmed; but it's a start and gets you moving, which is a big deal.

Start trying some healthier recipes today. You may not like the first few, and that's ok. Keep trying new ones til you find some that you really love.

Start applying for jobs today. You may not get chosen right away, but at least you're putting in the reps. Keep going til you line up interviews; then, if they don't pick you, learn from those interviews what you can improve on.

Start a dating site profile or go places to meet people today. You may not (and likely won't) meet the love of your life the first couple times, but keep trying and determine what works for you.

There's a lot of people out there still researching the perfect gym, the perfect recipes, the perfect job and career, still thinking about writing a book, and still wishing the love of their life would just show up. You know where they all are currently? They're still in the driveway. Get out of the driveway! You'll learn what you need to on the road, and past experiences and skills will come in handy in ways that you never even expected.

How are you preparing for your next goals?

____

____

How are you going to get out of the driveway today and start making progress towards your dream life?

____

____

Music

I often hear people say that they do not have time to learn new things that will help them on the journey to their dream life, or they never feel motivated enough. I mentioned before that we all have the same amount of time in the day, we just need to maximize that time as best as we can. One great way to do that (which I mentioned earlier) is changing what we listen to while we're driving. I want to discuss this more because it's such a simple change, yet can have a profound impact on our lives over time. Up until now, nearly everything else we've discussed has compared driving on a road trip to being on the metaphorical road to our dream lives.

This subject is something we're *literally* going to do while driving. How many times have you listened to the same songs in the car that, while making you feel good at the moment, do nothing for moving your life forward?

There's a couple of ways that we can take advantage of this time. First, choosing different music to listen to. Find songs that inspire and motivate you to take action towards your dreams. For me, I currently listen to a lot of NF, NEFFEX, Andy Mineo, Imagine Dragons, and The Score. Check these out; and if they don't do anything for you, keep searching until you find what does.

Another great way, like I've mentioned many times, is to listen to podcasts or audio books. These will give you not only the mindset, but can also give you the skillsets you need to take action.

My favorite podcasters currently are Ed Mylett, Trent Shelton, and Gary V. As for audio books, I personally prefer an actual book in my hands, but both can help a great deal. The important part is choosing books that help you move forward. Sure it may be relaxing to listen to Harry Potter, and I'm not saying you can't do that sometimes too (we all need chill time), but think about how much that's actually helping you toward your dream life. Think about things you want to learn, weaknesses that you feel you have, then listen to things that will help those areas.

Who are some artists that inspire and motivate you that you can listen to more often?

____

____

What podcasts or audiobooks will you start listening to? If you aren't sure, literally search for podcasts/audiobooks about ________.

____

____

Conclusion?

No, that's not a typo. I meant to put a question mark there. As long as we're breathing, our journey isn't over, correct? Even once we reach what we consider to be our dream life, there's likely still other goals that we have or come up with along the way. In order to stay at our destination, we also have to keep doing the things that got us there in the first place. This is where a lot of people seem to go wrong. We reach our goals, then think we're done. It's why people yoyo in their health. They diet and exercise to drop the weight, then once they get there, they go back to fast food and sitting on the couch. It may not be overnight, but it happens over time.

I hope that so far in this book, you've had some awakenings of things that are holding you back, realized some things that you need to change, and found some habits that you need to start (or stop) immediately. Here's where the rubber meets the road. Hopefully, you've already started making some changes while reading this; and if so, huge congratulations to you! If not, what will you do now? Will this just be another book that sits on a shelf and has no impact on your life? Or, will you start implementing some of what you wrote down to get closer to your dream life?

As mentioned, I've read a lot of personal development books; and while so many of them were amazing, I honestly can't tell you off the top of my head what I learned or changed based on most of them. I want this book to be different. I do not want this to be another book that sits on the shelf collecting dust. Because of that, there's one more chapter. I do not want you to read it right now, though.

Get out your phone, go to your calendar, and schedule a reminder or appointment for *six months* from today to read the last chapter. Yes, I know this isn't how conventional books are read. Who tells their readers to stop reading for six months? I'm doing this because without implementing what you've read and written, this book won't have any impact on your life. You're going to come back to this in six months and read the last chapter to review what you've changed, and the progress you've seen so far.

In the meantime, get to work!

Your dream life is waiting on you.

Your Six Month Tune Up

First of all, I want to congratulate you for taking the time to pick this book back up. It shows your commitment to fight for your dream life. Six months have gone by, and I hope that you've applied a lot of the action steps that you came up with previously. On a typical road trip, we sometimes need to look back and review how far we've come, what we've experienced, and (especially before we had GPS and only had paper maps) we needed to make sure we're still on the correct road.

In the past six months, I'm sure some life has happened. You've probably had some birthdays and holidays, maybe some anniversaries, or perhaps a vacation. You may have switched jobs, had relationship changes, or dealt with family drama or loss. You may have had some health scares or natural disasters as well. If you've been applying what you've learned, you've likely had some great wins, or you at least see them coming soon.

Now it's time to review the past six months.

What changes have you made in the past six months that have moved you down the road to your best life?

____

____

____

____

____

____

____

____

Now, go back and read the questions and your answers at the end of each chapter.

What other changes do you need to make over the next six months to make sure you get on/stay on the road to your dream life?

____

____

____

____

____

____

____

____

If at this point you're feeling a lot of guilt because you haven't applied any of what you've learned/written in this book, first I want you to give yourself some grace. Change is hard, and we all struggle with it. It's likely why you picked this book up in the first place.

Second, set another reminder, this time for *three* months from now. The best day to get into action was yesterday, but the second best day is today. Forgive your past. Stop making excuses for your future. You can do this.

Your dream life is waiting on you!

Let's Review

Below you'll find the title of each chapter and a brief summary of the topic discussed. I want you to keep these in your mind on a daily basis as a reminder to keep you on course:

Introduction

1. **Potholes & Speed Bumps**
   Trip and Land On Your Face & Humbling Moments

2. **Expressways & Cruise Control**
   Enjoy the Ride, But Do Not Forget the Habits That Got You There

3. **Distractions & Attractions**
   Rubbernecking & Small Wins Along the Way

4. **Wrong Turns**
   We Won't Always Choose the Right Path

5. **Traffic**
   People in the Way & Competition

6. **Accidents**
   We All Mess Up Sometimes

7. **Tolls**
   Investing the Work

8. **Construction**
   Tweaks & Updates to the Action

9. **How Long Is The Road?**
   Urgent in Your Action, Patient in the Result

10. **Destination Pictures**
    Print Them Out & Look at Them Regularly!

11. **Stay in Your Lane?**
    Glance Over to Get Ideas, But Don't Let It Derail You

12. **I Set the Path, You Set the Pace**
    I Can Guide You, But You Have to Put the Work In

13. **More Than One Road**
    Be Ready to Change Roads When Needed

14. **GPS**
    Make Sure You Have the Right Guidance

15. **Are You Steering The Vehicle?**
    Who's in Control?

16. **Keep Your Eyes on the Road**
    Stay Focused

17. **Passengers**
    Who's in the Car with You?

18. **Lonely Night Time Roads**
    Sometimes the Journey is Scary

19. **You Can't Drive On E**
    Self Care is Required

20. **Weather The Storms**
    Do Not Let Them Make You Turn Around

21. Bathroom Breaks
Pause, Reset, Get Moving Again

22. Hills
Maintain the Uphill Habits on the Downhills Too

23. Road Rage
Keep Your Cool

24. Terrain
There's Different Speeds We Need to Take Sometimes

25. Kids In The Back Seat
Remember: They Don't Always Listen to What We Say, But They Watch What We Do

26. Gas Mileage
Fuel Efficiency
Make Sure You Have the Proper Habits in Place

Pushing The Car
Discipline When The Gas Isn't There

27. Vehicle Health
Take Care of the Only One You Have

28. Rear View Mirror
Learn from the Past, But Do Not Let It Distract You from the Present & Future

29. Car Lights
Turn Signal
Share Where You're Headed with Others

Made in the USA
Middletown, DE
22 August 2024